What Shape is She in?

What Shape is She in?
A Guide to the Surveying of Boats

Allan H. Vaitses

International Marine Publishing Company   Camden, Maine

Published by International Marine Publishing Company

10 9 8 7 6 5 4 3

Copyright © 1985 International Marine Publishing Company

Library of Congress Cataloging in Publication Data

Vaitses, Allan H.
  What shape is she in?

  Includes index.
  1. Boats and boating — Inspection.   I. Title.
  VM321.V358   1985   623.8'2023   84-48689
                      ISBN 0-87742-192-7

International Marine Publishing Company offers software for sale. For information and a catalog, please contact TAB Software Department, Blue Ridge Summit, PA 17294-0850.

Questions regarding the content of this book should be addressed to:

International Marine Publishing Company
Division of TAB Books, Inc.
P.O. Box 220
Camden, ME 04843

Typeset by The Key Word, Inc., Belchertown, MA
Printed and bound by BookCrafters, Chelsea, MI
Illustrated by Jim Sollers

Contents

Preface *vii*

1 Introduction *1*

2 The Nuts & Bolts of a Survey *7*

3 Surveying a 30-Foot Fiberglass
IOR Production Auxiliary Sloop *18*

4 Boat Pox *44*

5 The Mislaid Deck *49*

6 The Moribund Ones *54*

7 Imported Boats *69*

8 Sap from Fiberglass? *77*

9 Part by Part: What to Look for
in a Fiberglass Boat *88*

10 Part by Part in Wood *151*

Index *162*

Preface

Writing this book was almost inevitable, for, like the Ancient Mariner's voyage, my adventures in surveying have left me with a compulsion to relate them. Of course, physically, surveying is not much to tell about. It is a blue-collar job in which one must be willing to make close contact with muddy ground, antifouling paint, dead or dying marine life, and such apparel-tearing, oil-and-grease-bearing areas of the interior as the lazarette, engine space, bilge, head, and rope locker, among others.

Intellectually, however, surveying can be intriguing enough for anybody. It calls for the evaluation of an always different combination of structure, hardware, and equipment, which may be new or very old. Sometimes it will tax the expertise of the most knowledgeable in boat construction. At all times it entails as much responsibility as anyone could want, and more than one without a thorough knowledge of the trade ought to assume—except, perhaps, for his own account.

That last sentence is definitely a warning. In these times, when at the slightest imagined damage citizens unleash the law against one another in civil suits, even the best-qualified, most careful, and—hopefully—well-armored surveyor risks being "taken," while one with limited experience could easily become the sitting duck in a shockingly unchristian shakedown.

Intellectually, then, surveying is like performing on a high wire. It demands training and concentration, and it has a fascination that is intensified by danger. The first part of this book is largely anecdotal in the hope of conveying some of that fascination, which includes but is not limited to the pleasure of looking over good work, of unraveling a boat's problems, and the sport of threading one's way between broker, owner, boatyard personnel, buyer, and well-meaning "expert" friends who attend the survey—keeping one's perceptions clear of their influence, as a hockey player does the puck, until it can be delivered to the goal, which is the survey report.

The last part of the book lists parts of the boat that must be studied and describes the more common problems to look for, so that anyone interested in trying his hand at surveying will have an outline with which to work. Whether the reader intends to do that, or is simply interested in a better understanding of what's involved in a survey, I hope he will find this book helpful and enjoyable.

Thanks to Robert N. "Bobby" Kershaw, surveyor, who taught me much about the trade; to J. Richard "Dick" Sciuto, broker, for generous advice; and to grandchildren Allan II, Stephen, Jr., and Allayne, who often took notes patiently while "Grump" prowled around a boat.

1

Introduction

This is a book about the surveyor's trade, about wooden and fiberglass boats I have surveyed, and—indirectly—about their owners, buyers, brokers, designers, and builders. In writing it, my objectives are to help the prospective buyer eliminate many boats from consideration on his own, without the expense of a professional survey; to give him enough knowledge of the surveyor's trade to judge when a surveyor has or has not done his job well; and to get an owner better in tune with the progressive maintenance needs of his boat.

Although I have not knowingly left out any important details of how one goes about doing a survey, no one, unless already steeped in boatbuilding, should expect to become a professional surveyor merely by reading this book. A surveyor must be familiar with every part of a boat and how it is all put together. He should also know what the most common faults and failures are and how to recognize them, although, as technology changes, he will be confronted with ever new forms of deterioration. These things are not quickly learned, and that is why the people best able to work into surveying without a long apprenticeship are those with long experience in boatbuilding.

Not that only professionals get the kinds of experience needed in surveying. Many amateurs maintain, repair, rebuild, or build their own boats, either because they enjoy doing so or because they cannot afford to take the work to a boatyard. Some of these folk learn much of what a surveyor must know.

I hope this book will make more sailors aware of the importance of a careful survey, a very basic importance stemming from the fact that boats live in the water, which, as Joseph Conrad said, is always stealthily awaiting a drowning. The most crucial surveys, I suppose, are those of boats subject to a high-risk use such as offshore racing, cruising, fishing, or carrying passengers for hire. Financial risk, too, while not as critical as that of life and limb, increases the surveyor's worries. The buyer's bottom dollar plus a large debt may be riding on a survey.

I will not soon forget a young fisherman whose newly acquired but ancient dragger, coming in with a full fish hold, suddenly went to the bottom of the channel. When raised, she was found to have opened up amidships in way of the hold. A few square feet of ceiling and ribs were so rotten that one could tear chunks out with his bare hands. Despite enough hull insurance to get her back into service, the young owner lost so much fishing time to repairs and repeated breakdowns of the engine, which never fully recovered from its saltwater dunking, that he could not keep up his mortgage payments and lost the boat. If only the surveyor had found that rotten patch, what a difference it might have made in his young client's career!

Yet the prospect of a life's savings or a career hanging in the balance can hardly shake up a surveyor more than a buyer who announces that he wants an older boat to sail to South Africa or Buenos Aires. I had a client headed for each of those places in one recent year, along with the usual number intending to live aboard or to range the East Coast and the Caribbean Sea. Incredibly, the only boat that the buyer bound for South Africa could afford was one whose former owners had despaired of trying to rebuild. What did I do? There was little for it but to turn teacher and outline the needed rebuilding work in my report. But despite the best recommendations I could muster, my report was submitted to this hardy soul with grave misgivings.

Suppose you are the usual fair-weather, weekend yachtsman who is trading up to a somewhat bigger, better-equipped, or more comfortable boat. Do you need a survey? I would say that, starting at a length between 18 and 24 feet and a price of $3,000 to $5,000, you do, unless:

(1) You are very familiar with the type of boat you are buying—how it is built and what its usual problems are.

(2) The money involved is not that important to you, and you can well afford any repairs that might be needed.

(3) You are not going to insure the boat. (Insurance companies usually require a survey, and if there must be one, why not get it *before* you buy?)

(4) You are not going to borrow money using the boat as collateral. (Lenders usually require a survey, and they almost always require insurance, with *its* requirement of a survey.)

The cost of a survey is modest. It currently averages between 1 and 2 percent of the value of the boat, although it is usually based not on value but on the size and complexity of the boat and its distance from the surveyor's place of business. My 1984 fee schedule, which I believe was representative, was $6 per foot for boats up to 30 feet long, $7 per foot for 30- to 40-footers, and $8 per foot for 40- to 50-footers. Boats larger than 50 feet entail such high and variable levels of complexity that I find it best to negotiate the fee on a case-by-case basis. Long travel time (say, greater than one hour) is usually reflected either in the fee or in a reimbursement for expenses. It is not unusual for a surveyor to be flown across the country or overseas to survey an extremely expensive vessel, with travel and lodging being paid by the client. In any case, given the least doubt about a boat's condition, a survey is an excellent investment. If a boat is in obviously questionable condition, the prospective buyer can even arrange a very inexpensive "preliminary survey," essentially an initial once-over to tell him whether putting down that deposit and paying for a full survey is warranted.

When you hire a surveyor, how do you find a good one? How do you tell whether he's doing a good job? How do you get rid of him if he appears to be incompetent? That tough trio of questions was raised by the editors early in our discussions of this book. I'll tackle the last two first, because they have no really satisfactory answers. Fortunately, if a good surveyor is found, they need none.

In order to make an early, accurate judgment on the quality of a surveyor's work, a buyer would need a fair bit of knowledge and experience himself. More usually, buyers do not find out whether a survey is a good or bad one until after the boat has been bought or rejected, presumably on the basis of the report. That is just a bit late, and if this book can provide a basis to discriminate between good and bad surveys *before* a prospective buyer makes his choice, or an insurer writes the policy, or a lender makes the loan—then it will have been a worthwhile project.

Getting rid of an incompetent surveyor could be problematical. In hiring him to survey the boat, a buyer is making a verbal contract to pay the surveyor's fee. Therefore, while cutting the survey short would be as easy as saying you don't want him to go on with it, any attempt on your part to prorate his fee could become a sticky business. Unless a mutually satisfactory agreement on a partial amount can be reached, it might be less trouble in the long run to pay the full fee and write it off as the cost of not getting stuck with a bad survey.

Of course, finding a good surveyor will take care of the other two questions. So it is well worth the effort. You *can* find one, but you need the recommendations of people who have experience with the surveyors in your area. Such people would be, in increasing order of their familiarity with surveyors: other boating people, boatyard operators, marine insurance agents, and boat brokers. Of the first two, a boatyard operator sees more surveyors than a yachtsman normally would, being involved, however casually, with almost every survey done in his yard. In time, he is bound to know something about the local surveyors.

All boats on which agents write insurance and most of the boats a broker sells are "subject to survey," so people in these two occupations know more surveyors and more about the quality of their work than anyone else. I see an insurer's acquaintance as being narrower in that the danger of loss is his main concern. It is also somewhat indirect in that the agent usually puts a binder on the boat, gets the owner to have a survey done, then submits the survey to the insurance company for approval and issuance of a policy.

Boat brokers, on the other hand, are alert to every facet of a survey because of its effect on the prospective buyer and the tentative sale.

Theoretically, there is a conflict of interest whenever a broker recommends a surveyor. He would like to sell the boat. Will he, therefore, tend to recommend surveyors who will be easy on her and avoid mentioning those known to be uncompromising? Some short-sighted characters might do so. No reputable broker, however, would want to be in the position of both having arranged the sale of the boat and having recommended the surveyor should grievous unreported or misdiagnosed faults be discovered after the boat changes hands.

In any case, brokers recommend surveyors to clients every day. They often name several, there being safety in numbers, but they may identify one surveyor on the list as the best to survey a particular type of boat or construction. If anyone knows who that would be, a broker does.

Before hiring a surveyor, I would not hesitate to ask him about his qualifications. If he knows his business, he certainly won't mind, and it is a signal to him that you really want the boat checked out, that you are not just going through the motions of having a survey done. I would favor a surveyor who is long on experience, but I would not be impressed by a formal title, a fancy logo, or letters after his name indicating membership in societies. Those displays indicate nothing about ability, only ostentation, gregariousness, and, quite likely, insecurity.

Neither would government regulations and licensing of surveyors make it any easier to differentiate between good surveyors and bad. Invariably when an occupation is regulated "for the protection of the public," it soon becomes a government-enforced monopoly complete with high prices and entrenched incompetence. Government intervention couldn't turn a bad surveyor into a good one any more than the possibility of being sued for damages can. (Despite the fact that most surveyors append to each survey a disclaimer paragraph like the one I show on page 43—a virtual necessity in our highly litigious society—surveyors can be and have been held financially liable for their findings.)

Judging the quality of a surveyor's work, either when (and if) you attend the survey or when you read the report, is going to be very difficult unless you are fairly knowledgeable and observant yourself. Even if you are pretty sharp, and you think he is not, it might pay to be a little patient. A surveyor who seems to be napping may be deep in thought, and some of us are, I trust, not goofy so much as absent-minded. I'd rather not hear what some people probably say when they watch me lie in a cockpit locker or a quarter berth for 10 or 15 minutes just looking and poking at the engine, tank, steering, and other systems. If a surveyor can get the buyer to crawl in there and then start reeling off a list of items that he should know about and inspect from time to time for one kind of failure or another, he'll realize that it's no place for dozing.

But then there was the time I reached down into an open hatchway in the cabin sole, heard something splash into the bilge, felt of the empty case in my shirt pocket, and said, "Damn! There go my glasses."

"No," said the buyer and the owner in unison. "You have them on."

2

The Nuts and Bolts of a Survey

I must confess that for me there are few jobs more pleasant than surveying a boat. It was not always so. In my youth I would have been quite bored by making a detailed study of most boats. Now, after a half century of boating and boatbuilding, the narrow boyish idealism that specifies this or that kind as the only good boat has given way to an empathy with all sorts of craft. Each model is an example of a different design and construction philosophy, and every survey is a study of how a boat built to a particular set of concepts is surviving. Fascinating as it may be, however, a survey is no lark. Human lives, along with whatever money is invested, are always at risk where boats are concerned. To point out when and how risks are heightened by infirmities or shortcomings in a boat is the underlying message of the surveyor's findings, his lonely responsibility, which at times fills him with anxiety and doubt.

By way of definition, surveys are done to determine a boat's condition, its safety, and its value. Being interwoven, these three aspects are all considered to some extent in every survey, but a surveyor will stress condition and the details of any needed repairs for a buyer, look more intently at the potential causes of accidents and disasters if the survey is ordered for or by an insurance

THE THREE BASIC TYPES OF SURVEYS

BUYER'S SURVEY

Purpose: Assess condition for prospective buyer. If buyer proceeds with purchase, copies are usually submitted to lender and insurer, often with a list of equipment appended for insurer.

Client: Buyer

Scope and Limitations: The most thorough type of survey with regard to structural features. Great detail on extent and seriousness of existing problems and on suggested repairs, as discussed throughout this book. Limitations: Most surveyors will not assess engine condition beyond what is visible externally or ascertainable from operation. Most surveyors will not assess sail condition in detail. Electronic gear, sails, etc. that have been removed for winter storage may not be inspected. Surveyor should note poor construction practices where visible (absence of bolts through toerail and hull-deck joint, absence of backing blocks for hardware, hardware of insufficient size, etc.), but cannot be expected to discover hidden flaws that have not yet caused problems (poor glue, absence of edge-to-edge fastenings in strip planking, etc.) if he does not have previous experience with that model of boat.

Expense: Discussed on page 3.

INSURANCE SURVEY

Purpose: Determine insurability. Required by insurance companies when boat is acquired and at periodic intervals thereafter.

Client: Buyer or Owner

Scope and Limitations: Greater emphasis on potentially hazardous features, though the buyer's survey will also note these. Less emphasis on structural features, nonhazardous flaws, and suggested repairs. Insurance companies require precise identification of all valuable gear such as electronics, even if stored away from the boat.

Expense: Same as buyer's survey.

APPRAISAL

Purpose: Establish boat's value preparatory to: (1) refinancing or a second mortgage; (2) setting a selling price; (3) donating the boat for a tax write-off.

Client: Owner

Scope and Limitations: Limited to setting a fair market value, with just enough description to back up the valuation, and to estimating how much the value will be increased by a projected rebuilding or refitting. General description, few details. Often done by brokers alone or in association with surveyors. Not all surveyors do appraisals.

Expense: Much less than a buyer's survey.

company, or try to get the most accurate possible handle on costs and fair market value if the report is going to a mortgagee. The scope and limitations of these three general types of surveys are summarized in the accompanying table.

Except for such emphasis on the particular client's needs, possibly with the respective designation of the report as "Buyer's Survey," "Insurance Survey," or "Appraisal," all surveys necessarily cover the same items. Literally, they include every detail of the boat affecting its condition, safety, and value. In the few hours allotted, a surveyor must arrive at a judgment concerning all parts of the craft, even venturing some sort of opinion, advice, or caution about those that are out of reach and out of sight.

The recurring nightmare of a surveyor is that he has overlooked some item that will later turn out to be a serious flaw in the boat. Knowing that a slight lapse can bring momentous embarrassment, the prudent surveyor, like the prudent airplane pilot, is not above using a checklist to prompt his attention.

Many a surveyor will carry with him several printed pages of items to check off. In these, every part of a boat and type of gear is either named specifically or included implicitly under a more general heading, along with enough space to note its condition. At the end of the checklist, additional space is provided for general comments or summaries. These comprehensive forms also serve as reports. In an efficient sequence of events, the surveyor fills in a copy of the form on the job, adds his conclusions, and turns it over to his typist, who types it and mails it with a bill. The form accompanying this chapter is the one used by Robert N. Kershaw of Braintree, Massachusetts, and is possibly the most widely copied form in the yacht surveying business. It is included here in its entirety, although in practice the recommendations usually run onto additional sheets of paper. These recommendations cover everything from serious problems to very minor details, and there are sometimes as many as 50 or 60 of them. It is Kershaw's opinion that a form this detailed keeps the surveyor from cutting corners and ensures that he examines every aspect of the vessel.

Other surveyors take along a checklist or form but talk into a tape recorder as they study the boat. No doubt this is an efficient approach, too. One hazard, though, might be the inability of a typist to recognize and spell boatbuilding jargon, which may explain the "lifeline sanctions," "tow rails," "pressed hooks," and "mast callers" sometimes mentioned in surveys.

Do not conclude that a surveyor must work from a checklist in order to do his job properly. Forms don't work that well for me. After several attempts at a uniform, comprehensive form for my own use, I chucked the idea in favor of an outline or list to be checked just before leaving the boat. Only a few notes such as propeller and shaft sizes, engine serial numbers, or a brief reminder of a particular item or problem are made on this list, for I dislike interrupting the study of the boat to fill in a form. I also dislike being cramped for space under some headings in a form while leaving blanks under others, so I prefer to type out new pages for each boat. (If I were younger and expected to continue surveying boats long enough to make it worthwhile, I would probably buy a computer with a word processing program and a printer.)

I mention these different approaches only to illustrate that there is no one right surveying style. A comparative lack of gadgetry does not by itself indicate a poor surveyor. At the same time, equipment and helpers, animate or inanimate, don't make the man or the survey, and I have saved a copy of a 16-page survey, which, when it is put together with the facts about the subject boat, becomes a classic reminder of that axiom. Spoken into a recorder and impeccably typed, copied, and packaged along with a bill for $500, this buyer's survey wasn't worth the postage to mail it; its too many words described only what anyone could see. Perhaps the surveyor was preoccupied with his equipment, or perhaps he recoiled from intimate contact with the dirty bilges of the subject 50-year-old, 55-foot twin-screw motor yacht. Whatever the reason, he failed to note that, of the frame ends, the floor timbers, the top of the keel, and its cheekpieces, there remained *nothing* sound enough to hold the fastenings and caulking of the garboard strakes. Down the centerline on the inside, she had gone soft as a baked potato, with only her skin holding her shape. On the outside, the garboard seams had been covered full length with heavy battens fastened to the garboards and to the lower, harder part of the keel; incredibly, our beautifully outfitted and organized surveyor didn't bother to investigate this blatantly suspicious detail.

Three months later, another surveyor condemned the boat completely, saying that she was too far gone to be worth rebuilding. It was unfortunate that this man didn't do the first survey. He might have saved the buyer tens of thousands of dollars. Sad to say, coming when it did, this survey was worthless, too, for he was hired to do an appraisal that the buyer, now owner, could submit to prospective lenders. Obviously, it would have been a bit naive to submit a report saying the boat was not worth rebuilding, and this surveyor was more than naive if he thought the new owner would scrap the boat and throw away the scores of thousands he had invested in her.

One might ask why a surveyor shouldn't say a boat is worthless if that is what he thinks. In a buyer's survey he certainly should, but an appraisal is an entirely different situation. If an owner is having a boat rebuilt, the purpose of the appraisal is to advise the prospective lender on the current fair market value of the boat, to corroborate the amount of money the owner claims to have invested in the boat already, and to forecast the probable fair market value of the craft after the projected rebuilding. These are the numbers the lender needs in order to gauge the viability of a loan, for it is no secret that a lender wishes the borrower to have a substantial investment in the subject of the loan, and he prefers that the subject have, after the additional investment, a wide margin of value over the amount loaned.

Now, if the surveyor insists on calling the boat just about worthless, he could peg the current fair market value at scrap prices. But even in doing that he is ignoring the latest price posted in the market, the one established by the recent sale from a "willing seller to a willing buyer." To play it straight, he should base his appraisal on that price, modified perhaps by the book price for similar boats* and to some extent by his findings of poor condition. He cannot say,

---

Book prices for used production pleasure boats are given in the BUC book, published semiannually in two volumes by BUC Research (a division of BUC International), 1314 NE 17th Court, Ft. Lauderdale, FL 33305. At the time of this writing, Volume 1 ($55) covers boats built in 1977 through 1984; Volume 2 ($45) covers 1905 through 1976. The two volumes together cost $90.

however, that the boat is not worth rebuilding, for here is an owner already engaged in that. There is at least one individual who thinks the boat worth rebuilding, having put his money where his mouth is.

Again, despite some leeway in current value, his appraisal of the boat's probable value at the finish of the rebuilding should be strictly by the book. Which is to say, he should tell the banker as nearly as he can what a boat like this one is likely to bring in rebuilt condition.

Not to leave the anecdote unfinished, the owner of the motorboat hired a third surveyor to do a second appraisal. That one was probably more realistic, but before it could be submitted, a bank had already made the loan on the basis of the owner's personal creditworthiness. In effect, the banker was saying, "We don't care that much about what you're doing with the money, you have enough net worth and enough income backing it up to rate the loan with us."

Having discussed a buyer's survey and an appraisal, which were both less than satisfactory, it seems that something ought to be said about insurance surveys. Although I don't happen to know of any of these that have been unsatisfactory in the same sense, I have heard owners complain, at times, that through their recommendations, surveyors had forced owners to install safety equipment or make repairs they thought were unnecessary. Unfortunately, that's the surveyor's job, to report diligently those details that expose the craft and its occupants to potential accidents. Possible floodings, sinkings, fires and explosions, collisions, and men overboard concern an insurer most. Fortunately, the identification of hazards is a well-beaten path given the Coast Guard's *Rules and Regulations for Recreational Boats*, which is published annually (as a separate publication prior to 1980, but now as Subchapter S or Parts 173-183 of the *33 Code of Federal Registers, Parts 1-199)* and sold through the Superintendent of Documents, Government

On the following pages: *The survey form used by Robert N. Kershaw, Inc. The form is reproduced in its entirety, although the Recommendations would run onto additional pages.*

Robert N. Kershaw, Inc.

INCORPORATED

MARINE SURVEYORS & CONSULTANTS

EST. 1955

P.O. BOX 285 • BRAINTREE, MASSACHUSETTS 02184 • (617) 843-4550

PRIVILEGED and CONFIDENTIAL

YACHT SURVEY REPORT NO._____

Vessel Surveyed at_____Date of Survey_____

OWNERSHIP AND GENERAL DATA

Name of Vessel_____Registration No._____
Home Port_____Documentation No._____
Owner/Buyer_____ _____Address_____
Type of Vessel_____Where Built_____Year Built_____
Builder_____Max. Speed of Vessel_____
Builders Hull No. _____Does Owner Contemplate Chartering_____

VALUATION

Original Cost_____
Estimated Insurable Value_____
Estimated Replacement Cost_____

Condition as referred to in following data will be noted as: Excellent, Good, Fair, Poor
For RECOMMENDATIONS see last page of report.

HULL DETAILS – CONSTRUCTION

Length (O.A.)_____(W.L.)_____Beam_____Draft_____
Keel: Material_____Size_____Worm Shoe_____Condition_____
Frames: Material_____Size_____on centers. Condition_____
Ribs: Material_____Size_____on centers. Condition_____
Planking: Material_____Single or double thickness_____Condition_____
Decking: Material_____Thickness_____Condition_____
Deck beams: Material_____Size_____on centers. Condition_____
Fastenings: Material_____Condition_____
Joiner work: Material_____Condition_____
Topsides condition_____Below water line condition_____
Bilge Condition_____Sea cocks_____Condition_____

MACHINERY SPACE

Location_____Fuel Used_____
Engines: Single or Twin_____Make _____No. of cyls._____H.P._____each
Serial No. Starboard Eng._____Port Eng._____
Age_____Condition_____
Drip pan under engine_____Drip pan under carburetor_____
Backfire trap_____Type sediment bowls_____
Exhaust: Material_____Water cooled_____
    Clear of woodwork_____Condition_____
Shafting: Material_____Size_____Condition_____
Struts: Material_____Bearings_____Condition_____
Stuffing box: Material_____Condition_____
Propellers: Material_____Size_____Shoe under_____Condition_____

FUEL TANKS AND SYSTEM

Location of fuel tanks_____
Tanks: Material._____Number_____Capacity_____Condition_____
Manner of securing tanks_____Condition_____
Fill pipes: Tight to deck_____Located weather deck_____Condition_____
Tank vents lead overboard_____Condition_____
Fuel lines: Material_____Size_____Condition_____
Valves in fuel lines:_____Type_____Location_____Condition_____
Valve for drawing fuel below deck_____Condition_____

Robert N. Kershaw, Inc.

INCORPORATED

MARINE SURVEYORS & CONSULTANTS

Yacht Survey Report   Vessel _____

ELECTRICAL SYSTEM

Auxiliary generator: Make _____ Fuel _____ No. of Cyls. _____ H.P. _____
How cooled _____ Location _____ Condition _____
Electrical wiring: Material _____ Fused _____ Condition _____
Master switch: Type _____ Location _____ Condition _____
Batteries: Number _____ Volts _____ Location _____ Condition _____
Converter for shore supply: Type _____ Location _____ Condition _____
Bilge pump: Type _____ Location _____ Condition _____

HEATING UNITS

Type _____ Manufacturer _____
Location _____
Fuel _____ Fuel tanks _____ Valves _____ Condition _____
Woodwork properly protected _____ Duct Material _____ Condition _____
Automatic or manual control _____ Area covered _____

GALLEY

Location _____
Stove: Type _____ Fuel _____ Shut off valve _____ Condition _____
Woodwork properly protected _____ Condition _____
If L.P. gas system: Location of tank and regulator _____
Fuel lines: Material _____ Type tank _____ Condition _____
Water heater: Type _____ Fuel _____ Shut off valve _____ Condition _____
Refrigerator: Type _____ Electric of L.P. gas _____
Properly secured _____ Condition _____

VENTILATION

Engine compartment   Condition _____
Bilge blower _____ Full manual _____ Interlocked with ignition _____
Ducts _____ Number _____ Size _____ Extend to bilge _____

Fuel tank compartment

Ducts or vents _____ Number _____ Size _____ Condition _____

Galley

Provision for venting stove _____
Opening ports _____ Condition _____

FIRE FIGHTING EQUIPMENT

Portable extinguishers: Number _____ Condition _____
Type extinguisher _____ Location _____ Date charged _____
_____   _____   _____
_____   _____   _____
Built-in system: Make _____ Type _____ Area covered _____
Manual or automatic system _____ Date weighed _____ Condition _____
Bilge fume detector: Make _____ Condition _____

ELECTRONIC AIDS

Radio ship to shore: Make _____ Size _____ Condition _____
Radio direction finder: Make _____ Condition _____
Depth sounder: Make _____ Condition _____
Automatic pilot: Make _____ Condition _____
Ground plate _____ Condition _____

GROUND TACKLE

Anchors: Number _____ Kind _____ Size _____ Condition _____
_____   _____   _____
Anchor line: Size _____ Length _____ Kind _____ Condition _____
_____   _____   _____
Mooring: Weight _____ Type _____ Pennant _____ Size _____ Condition _____
Location and supervision of mooring: _____
Is mooring considered adequate _____

Robert N. Kershaw, Inc.

INCORPORATED
MARINE SURVEYORS & CONSULTANTS

Yacht Survey Report   Vessel _____

SAILING YACHTS

Number of Masts: _____ Rig: _____

Spars and masts: Material _____ Hollow or solid _____ Condition _____

Sails: Material _____ Number _____ Age _____ Condition _____

_____ _____ _____ _____

_____ _____ _____ _____

_____ _____ _____ _____

_____ _____ _____ _____

Standing rigging: Material _____ Age _____ Condition _____

Running rigging: Material _____ Age _____ Condition _____

Center board or keel: Material _____ Draft-board down _____ Condition _____

WINCH INVENTORY

SHEET WINCHS	MAIN MAST WINCHES	MIZZEN MAST WINCHES
Primary _____	_____	_____
Secondary _____	_____	_____
Jib _____	_____	_____
Main _____	_____	_____
_____	_____	_____

TENDERS AND MOTORS

Make _____ Length _____ Year Built _____ Value _____ Condition_____

Motor: Make _____ H.P. _____ Year Built _____ Value _____ Condition_____

RECOMMONDATIONS:

Comments:

Surveyor

Printing Office, Washington, D.C. 20402; the American Boat and Yacht Council's *Standards and Recommended Practices for Small Craft* (write to ABYC, P.O. Box 806, 190 Ketcham Avenue, Amityville, NY 11701); and the National Fire Protection Association's Publication No. 302, *Fire Protection Standards for Pleasure and Commercial Motor Craft*, 1984 edition (NFPA, Batterymarch Park, Quincy, MA 02269), to name perhaps the primary such guides.

An insurer also needs some verification of the inventory of gear and equipment, complete with serial numbers whenever possible, so that he will know what he is insuring, or, after the loss, what he *did* insure.

Of course, the condition of a boat affects its accident-proneness; further, an insurer needs to know the fair market value, insurable value, and replacement value (the latter being what a new, identical boat would cost).

An insurance survey, then, is more involved than an appraisal and must be almost as detailed as a buyer's survey. This brings us full circle to the buyer, who is still king. He can use every bit of information the surveyor can put together for him, for he is likely to use the survey not only as a guide in purchasing the boat, but to obtain a loan and insurance for it as well. Furthermore, in every buyer's survey, he pays the bill.

What tools do I carry in my canvas surveying bag? Not nearly as many as some surveyors do, but perhaps more than some others. Three items essential to the trade are a flashlight, a probe, and a hammer.

The flashlight is so important that I carry two, sometimes even three. The probe might be a pocketknife or an ice pick. One young surveyor I met was using an oyster knife, and I must say that its spring-temper steel blade allowed him to hammer it into fiberglass and wood and pry them open in a manner that would snap other tools. Not that I recommend anyone doing *that* without the owner's permission! My own favorite probe is a small, slender screwdriver of good-quality steel, preferably one with a tough plastic handle so that it can double as a hammer or mallet for sounding.

Sounding—tapping with a hammer—is the quickest and least destructive way to locate rot obscured by paint, and also to determine whether layers of fiberglass or of laminated wood are separating. When one taps his way off solid wood onto wood softened by rot, the resonance of the sound will disappear. Solid, one-piece material makes a single, relatively clear note; delaminated material makes a cracked or double note.

Other tools I like to have along are several additional sizes of screwdrivers, a couple of adjustable wrenches, plain and water-pump pliers, and a mirror. With these tools one can take out sample bolts and screws; remove screw-fastened panels; open stubborn bunker and deck plates, lift-outs, and hatches; and take apart almost anything that needs to be gotten out of the way. And if you can't get your eye lined up for a look into some area, the mirror will sometimes give you a squint at it.

About the only other tool I always carry is a rule to measure propellers, shafts, and other items, as surveyors often must. But I don't carry chalk, crayon, or felt-tip markers because I haven't figured out what advantage there is in drawing circles around each defect, as some surveyors do. Marks on the boat won't be much help when I'm miles away writing my report. Besides, if the boat isn't sold, why tip off the competitor who surveys her next?

3

Surveying a 30-Foot Fiberglass IOR Production Auxiliary Sloop

On a fine morning in mid-May, I turned my pickup through the gates of a Rhode Island boatyard and marina and cruised slowly down the road between the bulkhead, with its boat-lined finger piers, and the rows of boats still sitting out in winter storage. One moment searching for the 30-foot sloop I was there to survey, the next moment admiring the boats newly launched, I would have been a menace on a more traveled street. Yet what lifelong boatman doesn't lose himself in the panorama of a boatyard? Besides, to me, relishing such scenes is one of my rewards for surveying boats.

Coming upon a nameless 30-foot sloop that fitted the location and description given by the buyer, I parked the truck near her, walked to the marina office, made my mission known, confirmed the boat's identity, picked up the keys, and inquired about a ladder for getting aboard. The owner-manager was congenial and accommodating, although already slipping into that dazed condition by which, unconsciously, boatyard operators protect their sanity in the midst of the spring launchings. "Looks as though the spring rush is on," I ventured.

"Rush, yes; spring I haven't had time to notice. Give a shout if you need anything."

Leaning the ladder against the boat, I set down my canvas bag containing a few basic tools, two flashlights, and a clipboard, and began studying the exterior of the hull. The gelcoat on the topsides was in excellent condition. Well, on a one-year-old boat it ought to be. Not a single anchor ding on her bows. That could indicate the use of slips and moorings more than anchoring, or perhaps daysailing and racing, mostly, and very little if any cruising.

A faint waterline of color change in the bottom paint indicated where she floated when at rest. It was well below the painted line, roughly parallel to it, and at about the same level on both sides amidships. I concluded from this evidence, plus a short trip out ahead of her to eyeball the alignment of the fin keel with the stem, that the keel was fitted up straight on this boat. They aren't always so. A 26-foot boat by the same builder that I had surveyed not a year before was fresh in my memory.

Studying the spade rudder on that 26, I had seen that it didn't line up with the keel. I thought initially that it might have a bent stock, which sometimes happens. A Travelift prevented me from backing off for a better view from astern, so I had gone out forward of the boat, where I was shocked to see how far to starboard the keel was canted. Checking the flotation waterline against the painted one and measuring from the bottom of the keel to the rail on either side bore out by an inch and a half what was apparent to the eye. When I climbed aboard I could see that the top surface of the hull recess into which the flange at the top of the cast iron keel bolted was itself tilted. Yet all surrounding fiberglass was solid, and the keel bolts were tight. These circumstances could only mean that the keel had been bolted into a green hull too soon after layup, that the keel and hull were not carefully leveled, and that the hull had then cured at this tilt. Certainly the hull hadn't been molded that way. No production builder is likely to use a hull mold with a cockeyed keel recess.

Anyway, nothing of that sort had happened to this 30-footer's fin keel. What about damage from grounding? Inspection of the leading edge and bottom of the fin gave no hint of such, but that was hardly conclusive. A crucial place to look for damage from striking one of these short fin keels is just forward of and abaft where it joins the hull. A rock or hard bottom, in stopping the bottom of the keel while the hull's forward momentum continues, causes the keel to try to

rotate up into the hull aft and down out of it forward. The depth of these keels usually being considerably greater than their fore-and-aft length, the forces involved are enormous, and the hull laminate is often broken in a thwartships line at one or both ends of the keel. Careful inspection of those areas is important on any fin-keel boat.

Although there were no breaks evident in the laminate at the ends of the keel on this boat, there were fine cracks in the keel sides about 10 inches below the hull where the fiberglass structure or stub keel and the lead casting were bolted together. These were cracks in the fairing putty, nothing structural. Fiberglass is more flexible than putty, and putty often cracks when the fiberglass bends. Nevertheless, I made a mental note: When aboard the boat, I would inspect the bilge and whatever reinforcements were used over the keel for signs of stress or damage alongside the keel or at either end. Why? Because I had seen boats which, despite having no readily ascertainable damage on the outside, had some bad breaks in their internal reinforcements.

In an IOR sloop like this one, the reinforcing members are often a separately laminated section containing floor timbers and fore-and-aft stringers in a one-piece grid resembling an oversized waffle. Laid up in its own mold off the boat, this structure is then fiberglassed down in the bilge over the keel. The keel is bolted through it, and the top of the "waffle" often supports the cabin sole. I was once called upon to study one lightly built racing boat in which several of the athwartships, floor timber–like members over the after end of the keel had been broken, undoubtedly when the boat struck ground and the keel pushed up sharply against them. The breaks, however, were not discovered until the canoe body of the hull settled around the keel during winter storage. After witnessing a few such cases of internal injury, one learns never to trust outward appearances entirely, no matter how perfect.

It being my habit to walk around the boat several times on the

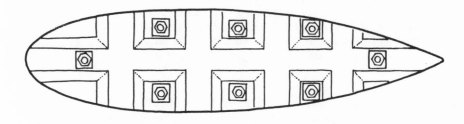

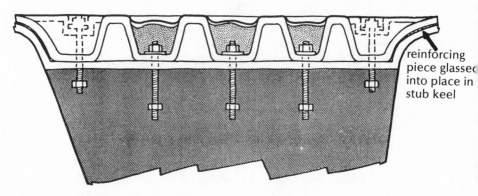

reinforcing piece glassed into place in stub keel

A longitudinal section through the one-piece reinforcing waffle of a fiberglass sailboat with canoe body, stub fiberglass keel, and lead fin keel. Covering the bolt heads with goop seals out moisture and extends the working lifetime of the bolts. Not shown here are the scuppers with which all the "floor timbers" should be provided.

outside, I took stock of the through hulls on the next circuit. There was what seemed to be the engine intake, a bronze through hull just to one side of where the engine would be located. If so, she must have a small engine, for it was only a ⅜-inch IPS (iron pipe size) fitting. I noted that there was not the customary scoop strainer over it. On the centerline forward of the keel was a plastic speedometer through hull, and nearby was a depthfinder unit. It was curious that these three items were the only fittings through the hull underwater. The others were all in the transom and above the waterline with the boat at rest: two cockpit scuppers and a bilge-pump through hull, all Delrin, a chrome-plated bronze vent, undoubtedly for the fuel tank, and an exhaust fitting of stainless steel tubing with a welded flange. Missing were toilet through hulls of any description.

On the following pages: *On a lightly built racing boat I once surveyed, the impact of a grounding had produced enough torque in the keel to break several "floor timbers" in the reinforcing piece. When the boat was hauled for the winter and stored with most of her weight bearing on the keel, the hull slumped on either side, widening the cracks in the floor timbers and distorting the boat's shape. I recommended that the boat first be jacked up and allowed to regain her shape with more load-bearing support up around the hull; then the floor timbers were to be covered by an added laminate at least ¼-inch thick that would continue several inches either side of the timbers before tapering off in thickness. Alternatively, if it were preferred not to raise the cabin sole even slightly, the old tops of the floor timbers could be ground off entirely and replaced. It would be necessary in this case to fill the hollow timbers, creating a form for the new laminate. This boat's keel had another, chronic problem, one springing from the fact that only the forward part of the keel was lead, while the after part was a hollow fiberglass shell rabbeted and fastened into the lead. Cradle blocks under both the solid and the hollow parts had caused the rabbeted seam to work loose and leak. The solution was to fill the seam with epoxy or Marine-Tex, reinforce it with either machine screws or stainless self-tapping screws, and in the future, to place no cradle blocking under the hollow fiberglass shell.*

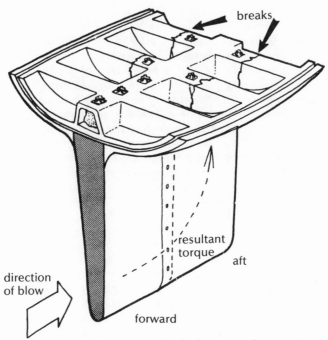

breaks

resultant torque

aft

direction of blow

forward

Breaks in a one-piece or "egg crate" reinforcing part caused by a hard impact.

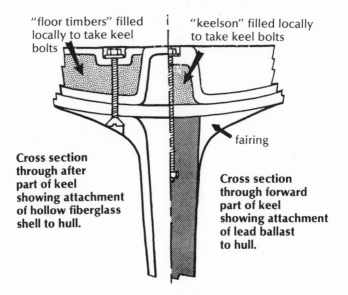

"floor timbers" filled locally to take keel bolts

"keelson" filled locally to take keel bolts

fairing

Cross section through after part of keel showing attachment of hollow fiberglass shell to hull.

Cross section through forward part of keel showing attachment of lead ballast to hull.

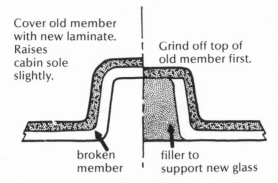

Cover old member with new laminate. Raises cabin sole slightly.

Grind off top of old member first.

broken member

filler to support new glass

Two alternative repairs to the broken members.

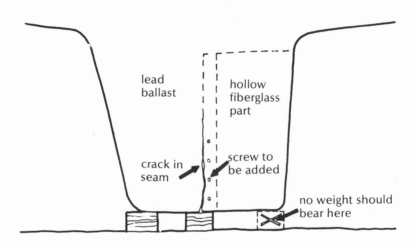

lead ballast

hollow fiberglass part

crack in seam

screw to be added

no weight should bear here

I turned next to the propeller, a 13-inch (diameter) by 8-inch (pitch) folding Martec on a ¾-inch stainless steel shaft supported by a bronze strut with a rubber bearing insert. Shaking the shaft revealed no play or rattle in the rubber bearing. One would expect as much after one season's use, but of the boats over five years old that

I have surveyed, about half have been in need of a new rubber insert. The propeller was tight on the shaft and in "like-new" condition, and the shaft showed no eccentricity or wobble when turned. The strut had a four-bolt base set into a recess. None of the bronze was pitted or even discolored, which took the edge off my discovery that there were no sacrificial zincs on this boat. Nevertheless, in these times of high shore-current usage at marinas as well as ever-increasing use of ship's power, it is hardly safe to assume that from one year to the next a boat will continue to show no electrolytic problems just because it has a minimum of metal parts and dissimilar metals underwater. One should keep an eye out for signs of destruction by impressed currents.

The transom-mounted rudder looked and felt quite substantial. Deep and narrow, hanging well below the transom without a skeg, it would need to be strong. A friend who worked for this boat's builder had once shown me the room where they produce their rudders and centerboards. A hinged two-piece mold is constructed for each model of rudder or board. A fiberglass skin or shell for each half of the part is laid up in its half of the mold, and any internal metal parts such as a rudder stock are set in place; then the mold is filled and clamped tightly shut until the resin cures. The key to the success of parts so constructed is the mix of resin and reinforcing materials used in the core. Core strength may be supplemented somewhat by the ruggedness of the skin or shell, but because of the joint all the way around the centerline, the shell's ability to hold the halves together is limited. I must say that the cores used by different companies to build their rudders vary widely, from materials that have virtually no physical strength, such as polyurethane foam, through tougher cores such as Airex foam, wood, or metal stiffeners, to relatively dense, hard cores made like this company's with casting resin and reinforcing fillers. There are also custom rudders, produced by a different technique in which a shaped wood, foam, or composite core is hand wrapped with a fiberglass laminate; when done properly, these are the best of all because of the continuity of their skin.

One can get some idea of the sturdiness of a rudder by tapping it with a small hammer or other hard object to sound out its solidity and density, by locking its helm and tugging on the blade to see how

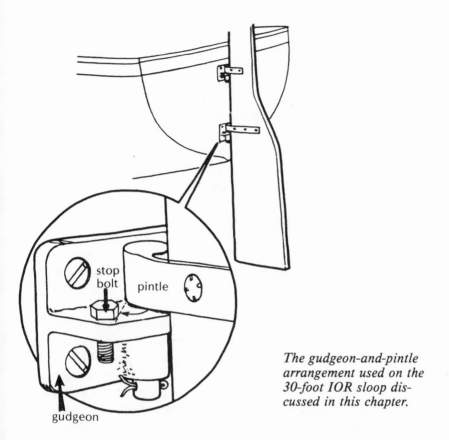

The gudgeon-and-pintle arrangement used on the 30-foot IOR sloop discussed in this chapter.

it resists twisting (which is, after all, its purpose), and by hefting it if possible to estimate its weight. The thing to remember is that almost all production rudders are molded in two pieces, and those lacking a dense core without internal voids will very likely be split, if they winter in a freezing climate, by water that penetrates and then freezes inside them. I could not remember having seen a rudder by this builder that had been split by ice. Nevertheless, from habit, I inspected this one carefully along the centerline and around the bottom, especially. Its condition was very good except for a small patch at the lower pintle. I reasoned that the damage there was undoubtedly inflicted by excessive pressure of the stainless steel pintle fitting against the stop bolts with which the gudgeon, also of stainless, was fitted. An instance of backing into a pier or float, or possibly an excessive pressure bearing on the rudder when it was hard over, had caused the pintle to crush the leading edge of the rudder. The pintle had been removed, straightened, and remounted over the patch, which was well done. The repair was only perceptible because of the faintly different hue a gelcoat patch almost always has, and the slight signs of rework on the pintle. Strong though stainless steel is, this particular hardware, which was new to me, seemed barely adequate for a rudder and boat of this size. With no skeg and only two sets of pintles and gudgeons holding the rudder by its top half, the pressures on them were bound to be enormous at times. The stops that kept the rudder from binding against the transom when hard over were bolts through holes in a horizontal web between the socket and mounting plate of the gudgeon; the pintle's strap would bear on a bolt when turned perhaps 35 degrees in either direction. The stop bolts were no more than 1¼ to 1½ inches from the axis of the pintle, and I could easily understand how that much leverage could generate enough pressure to crush the fiberglass and core inside the pintle's straps. The repair looked all right, but if it could happen once, it would happen again, unless something could be done to lessen that pressure. That is when I noticed that, although holes were there for them, no stop bolts had been installed in the identical upper gudgeon. "Aw, for Pete's sake!" I muttered to myself. "How come stop bolts were never installed in the other gudgeon? That would divide the pressure in half. And how come whoever repaired the rudder didn't notice they were missing? Oh well, my job is to recommend that they be put in, and that ought to do it."

I had now examined everything on the exterior of the hull and was making one last turn around the boat when the buyer and his wife arrived. It is not unusual for surveyors to react negatively when the buyer wants to attend the survey. The main objection seems to be that the presence of anyone other than the surveyor, except possibly a helper, will distract him from his study of the craft and might sway or impair his judgment about what he finds. In my view, the buyer has always been welcome to participate, for a number of reasons.

First, everything the buyer can find out about the boat—everything I can point out, explain, discuss, or help him discover about her—can only improve his understanding of the problems or advantages he will inherit if he buys her.

Second, it is always easier and more effective to point out and explain items or conditions in situ than to write about them. Many laymen are not good at visualizing, and many do not understand boatbuilding jargon well. With both parties on the spot, the message will get through. Then, too, careful as he may be, no surveyor notices everything. I must confess that more than once the buyer has, wittingly or unwittingly, steered me to problems I might otherwise have overlooked.

Often, the sale of a boat must be confirmed, renegotiated, or aborted within but a few days, making it doubtful that the survey will reach the buyer quickly enough by mail. In that case, the surveyor will be committed to one or more lengthy conferences with the buyer to give him the sense of the report, so that he can make his decision. To me, this has always seemed at least as confusing or inconvenient as having the buyer along for the survey.

Finally, having the buyer at the scene is advantageous when a boat is found to have more extensive problems than the buyer is willing to assume. The survey can be aborted on the spot, saving everyone wasted motion, conferences, phone calls, and a formal report, which is a waste of both the surveyor's time and the buyer's money. Speaking for myself, I have no interest in writing a report for its own sake or for the money only, and I am more than happy to shave my fee when released by the buyer from the responsibility for completing a survey. (This usually cannot be done if the sale is consummated, because the buyer is then likely to need the survey for insurance and possibly for a mortgagee, and he should have it as a benchmark of the boat's condition at the time he purchased it. Further, if I may bring up an unpleasantness that sooner or later may fall into any life, the surveyor may someday need his report as a record of what he said about the boat should the buyer have trouble with her, and, thinking that the surveyor should have forewarned him of it, decide to sue.)

I was not at all unhappy, then, when the prospective owner and his wife arrived at the scene. They turned out to be young and personable, exuding an infectious excitement about their projected purchase. I launched a minitour of the exterior to explain what I had discovered so far. Up to this point, there was certainly little to tell that was negative. I had uncovered no damage, even superficial, and she was lacking only a scoop strainer for the engine intake, a sacrificial zinc for the bronze underwater fittings, and two stop bolts for the upper rudder gudgeon. Of these, only the stop bolts were a demonstrable necessity, unless, as I pointed out, there was no strainer in the cooling-water intake line, or unless at some future date the bronze began to show signs of electrolytic attack. That was great news to the buyers, and fine with me, too. A survey is just as important for what it finds faultless as for what faults it finds, and a survey that finds no serious problems is the best survey, the one that all parties to the sale are hoping for.

So it was in an upbeat mood that we filed up the ladder to extend the survey to her deck and interior. As I stepped on deck and glanced around, I could not suppress an "Oh, oh!," for the first irregularity to catch my eye was a darkened shadow along the joint between the teak toerail and the deck. That would be a clear silicone sealant. It could only mean leaks, and it ran the full length of the toerails on both their inboard and outboard sides.

"What's wrong?" asked Mrs. Kleinman.

"I don't know. We'll have to look below to see if we can find the leaks, but leaks there are. Otherwise, why would somebody take the trouble to try to seal off the area under the toerails with silicone?"

Unlocking the companionway and trooping below, we spread out to study the underside of the side decks for leaks. Whether due to an accent on racing or to a need to hold down the cost of this racer-cruiser model built at the 1980–81 peak of inflation, her interior struck me as surprisingly spartan for the price, but refreshingly open and uncluttered, too. Unlike the usual production boat of her type, the inboard surfaces of her hull and deck shells were not entirely obscured by liners. The deck joint, visible for its entire length, was of the type in which the deck fits into an inturned, rabbeted hull flange; the seam on deck was covered by the toerail. The seam belowdeck, where the inboard edge of the hull flange was overlapped by the deck laminate, was found by examination and probing to be solidly filled and glued together with a not-immediately-identifiable-but-seemingly-adequate substance. There

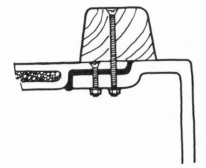

Hull-deck joint of the type used in the 30-footer in this chapter. Other joints are pictured in Chapter 9. Shown here are the stainless steel bolts that should have been used in the 30-footer.

were no signs that this deck joint, itself, was leaking. As I followed it along, however, it dawned on me that the usual row of regularly spaced stainless steel bolts or jagged, projecting points of tapping screws was missing. There were none of these, except where some piece of deck hardware—a lifeline stanchion or genoa track—was bolted through. In their stead, pop rivets were the only regularly spaced fastenings through the deck joint. By sending Mark on deck to locate the wooden bungs in the toerail, it was quickly established that these coincided with the rivets projecting below, and that the rivets were the only mechanical fastenings for both the toerails and the deck joint. Meanwhile, streaks on the interior sides of the hull and stains on the overhead were noticed, undeniable evidence that almost every one of the pop rivets had been leaking.

I chuckled with astonishment that the "big time" production builders of this boat had tried such a silly stunt, that a company bristling with engineering people would assemble a deck to a hull with glue of whatever kind and back up that connection with nothing but pop rivets, which were already overextended by the job of fastening a heavy teak toerail. It should have been obvious that the malleable pop rivets would stretch when the rails swelled, that the rails would loosen up as they shrank again, and that the rivets must finally leak down through the clearance holes made for them in the fiberglass. That was inevitable, but it was a bit startling to me to see it happening within a year. Perhaps not so obvious, but an ever-present, well-documented danger, was the possibility of the deck joint coming unstuck, in which case these pop rivets could not possibly keep it from gaping wide open.

That glued deck joints without strong backup fastenings can be treacherous I had learned from a 210 class sloop, the deck of which my shop had epoxy glued into a rabbeted hull flange using small aluminum pop rivets (like the rivets in this boat) without the usual husky backup bolts. The rivets were intended merely to hold the deck in place until the epoxy set. One afternoon, this long double-ender was leading the final downwind leg of a race when, at the urging of the backstay, the afterdeck peeled up like a sardine can lid. I've always wanted backup bolts (or some sort of stout fastenings) in deck joints since that incident. It cost me a trip to Maine in a pickup truck with two men, materials, tools, and a portable generator to get the job done on the mooring in one long day.

I explained to the Kleinmans that pop rivets of this size were not good fastenings for the toerails, and neither were they a good backup for the deck joint on this boat. They should be replaced with bolts. Preferably, the toerails should be taken up and rebedded at the same time, but at the least, each bolt replacing a pop rivet would need to be well bedded and made watertight, as with wicking and bedding compound under the washers. I speculated that if the manufacturer was apprised of this situation, it might possibly make repairs at no charge or at cost. It was even possible that the manufacturer was already involved in a recall to refasten the decks of this model. But whatever the attitude or position of the manufacturer, I explained that, as buyers, their next move was to advise the seller of this situation (one could as well bluntly remind him of it) and reach an agreement with him as to whether he was willing to make a price adjustment or talk to the manufacturer, as the original owner, about making repairs. Just for some numbers to work with, I suggested that a proper job done by a repair yard would probably cost from $1,000 to $2,000 but not more than $2,500. If the owner refused to adjust his price for this problem, claiming perhaps that it had already been allowed for, then they would have to decide whether to turn down the purchase of the boat or to accept it and assume responsibility for the repair themselves. In the latter case, a firm estimate for the repair would be a good thing to have in hand before closing the deal.

Being a creature of habit, I headed back up on deck as soon as the problem of the leaking pop rivets was outlined and resumed my standard survey itinerary. My fixed routine is to start on the ground (when the boat is hauled) and study the topsides and underbody first, then the deck, then the interior, and finally the parts that might be stored off the boat, such as spars, sails, and tender. In the interest of efficiency, I try always to follow this sequence so that each step is automatic and none is overlooked in preoccupation with some unusual feature, special problem, or sociable digression. My checklist and survey reports follow the same pattern for the same reason. In theory, this habit keeps the survey on autopilot and leaves the mind free to explore. On deck, I made the rounds, up one side and down the other, testing lifeline stanchions for solidity, examining every piece of hardware for its physical strength and its attachment to the deck (soon to be restudied from below for backing and for leaks), and studying the condition of the gelcoat, the fiberglass laminate, the wood trim, the portlights or cabin windows, the hatches, and the ventilators.* When it comes to detail, the hull of any boat is a desert compared to its deck.

The tiller and the top of the rudder could now be studied. There were some stress cracks in the rudderhead gelcoat where the tiller was fitted, and the bolt through the tiller had already loosened in the hole through the rudderhead. This made me wonder whether the boat was kept where constant wave action caused the rudder to rattle back and forth, whether the tiller had been a misfit and the rudder had had to be reamed out to get the bolt through it, or whether the bolt was simply never tightened up enough, which would quickly enlarge the hole. I would be recommending that the bolt be kept fairly tight (supplied with washers and cotterpins if necessary) and that, at some point, the rudderhead be either bushed or filled and rebored. I told the buyer that, knowing the construction of the rudder, I would consider the small stress cracks cosmetic unless they got worse in time; they were probably the result of a helmsman losing hold of the tiller while backing, causing the tiller to jam against the coaming as the rudder went hard over. One of the advantages of having the buyer along is that he can be given as much

---

*Chapter 9 is a part-by-part checklist of what to look for in a fiberglass boat.

detail as he can absorb—or his patience can bear—whereas written recommendations need to be brief.

The only other disturbing detail on deck was a pattern of stress cracks in the radius where the cockpit seat fronts turned into the sole. Stress cracks in the gelcoat are cracks that appear when it is stretched or compressed beyond its limits by overbending the laminate beneath it. Those created by a local impact tend to radiate from the area of contact, forming a "star crack," while those created by a bending or folding action tend to parallel the axis of the bend.

The cracks in this tub ran in and parallel to the turns between the sides and the bottom, and I concluded that these bends had been flexed beyond the gelcoat's endurance, probably by the weight of crew members jumping in and out of the tub. Since the tub was flanked by two quarter berths for most of its length, I went below and crawled aft in one of these to check out the construction. To see it all required unscrewing an access panel to the engine and tank space under the cockpit, but that would have to be done anyway in order to inspect the fuel tank, the forward part of the exhaust, and the propeller shaft stuffing box. As is often done, the cockpit sole had been reinforced with a core of end-grain balsa, but the tub sides or seat fronts, including the radius and a small margin around the bottom, were a not-too-thick single skin. There was no sign of cracking in the laminate itself. Now I knew at least that the laminate, being single, would be easily bent. Still, there was no way of knowing for sure whether the circumstances causing the stress cracks were normal or unusual. If by chance the cockpit tub had been subjected to extra-heavy trampling of a degree not likely to happen again, a simple sanding and gelcoat repair would suffice. On the other hand, a little additional fiberglass to beef up these corners wouldn't hurt, and it would be relatively easy to apply. So that's the way I told it and later wrote it up.

When surveying a deck, it is my habit to inspect the cockpit lockers and lazarette. In an aft-cockpit auxiliary sailboat, and especially in one made of fiberglass, this area holds more items of interest to the surveyor, which is to say more sources of potential trouble, than any other section of the boat. Here we find the cockpit scuppers and their hoses, through hulls, and seacocks (if any), often with seat drains, sink drains, and bilge pumps teed into them. We follow the engine exhaust line, independent bilge pump hoses if present, and possibly a tank vent line to their fittings in the transom or hull. Usually a fuel tank or two (and occasionally water tanks) will be here, with fill, vent, and supply connections and lines to be traced and checked for security, valves, and electrical grounding. An inboard rudder's port, stuffing box, and stock will be seen here, along with the boat's wheel steering system if she has one. The after end of the engine, if not also its flanks, must often be viewed or reached from the seat lockers or, as in this boat, from the quarter berths. This is the time and place to check out the propeller shaft stuffing box, the cooling-water intake, the shift-control linkage, and any other engine-related details not within reach or sight from the forward end of the engine.

As if these items are not enough, one will also find wiring for the stern light, the compass light, the bilge blower, possibly a whip or backstay antenna, and quite likely the engine instrument panel. Then, of course, there will be the engine shift and throttle controls and often a manual bilge pump mounted for cockpit operation. We must remember, too, that there should be ventilation of the engine and tank space with cowels, a blower, and hoses to the bilge; this ventilation is required by law if the fuel is gasoline, but it is also needed to dissipate heat and more importantly to facilitate the aspiration of diesel engines, which are very heavy breathers. Finally, this is often the best place to study the boat's construction, for here there are no liners and often no paint to hide the shells of the hull and deck. It is a good place to study the thickness of the laminates, the deck joint, and the bolting and backing plates of the deck hardware, more items of which may be located around the cockpit than on the rest of the deck. Wherefore, if one tires of looking down and around, he can look up at the fasteners in the overhead for the deck joint, toerails, lifeline stanchions and stern pulpit, chocks, cleats, turnblocks, winches, and genoa tracks. Of course, if the boat is a yawl or ketch, there will also be a mast step and partner and chainplates to look over.

No wonder then, that tight though these spaces often are, and usually filled to overflowing with all manner of sodden gear, it is a must in every survey to clear out the last fender, sail, awning, broken-handled rag mop, rusted can of engine oil, storm anchor, coil of line, hand bilge pump, life preserver, gallon of stove fuel, bag of charcoal briquettes, or outboard motor and portable tank, and then, if humanly possible, to wedge one's carcass flashlight in hand into each dank, slightly oily hole for a leisurely but hardly comfortable close-up inspection. The alternative is putting one's head in first, followed by as much of the body as is practicable (and extractable), but that can be so awkward that it is likely to make one hurry through his study and overlook something. Nothing is more frustrating than to pile all of the gear back into a locker and suddenly realize that one forgot to look at some crucial item such as a stuffing box or a seacock. Oh my, what ugly words come to mind. One soon learns that, in surveying, taking one's time saves time.

In the subject boat the bronze stuffing box was bright green with corrosion, more than enough evidence that it was weeping too freely. In a one-year-old boat, it wouldn't be likely to need repacking; just taking up the nut a bit would probably slow the drip. Aside from the stuffing box, everything in the engine and tank space seemed to be properly installed and devoid of rust streaks, leaking oil, or other indications of trouble. The engine was still winterized and the battery was off the boat, so no systems could be tried out. In such an event it is usual to hold a sum of money in escrow until the engine has been de-winterized and at least run a bit. Alternatively, the boat is launched and taken for a trial run before final payment is made. The former type of agreement was in effect on this boat, the buyers assured me. Meanwhile, the diminutive one-cylinder diesel, still all shiny and new looking, certainly didn't appear to have been abused, or even much used, in its one season.

The 8-gallon cylindrical aluminum fuel tank was mounted athwartships just abaft the engine, with its fill hose connected directly to a deck plate in the middle of the cockpit sole. Such an arrangement is not frowned upon when the fuel is diesel, but a wiser location for a gasoline fill plate is in the main deck, outboard of the coaming. The tank was well strapped down into fitted chocks. The fuel vent was high on the transom, and it, as well as the supply and return lines, was run with proper fuel fittings, hose, and valves.

The engine exhaust system was of the water-lift type, by far the most popular system in auxiliary sailboats for the past decade. The heart of the system is the water-lift muffler, a pot or cannister installed well below the level of the exhaust manifold and followed aft by a high loop in the exhaust line. Right after a downturned elbow on the manifold, water can be injected into the exhaust line, which can therefore be a single line (not water jacketed or lagged), made up of steam hose, if desired, right to the transom. The high loop keeps water that enters the line at the outlet from surging forward to the engine, and the pot serves as a low catch basin to collect and hold any water left in the system when the engine is shut down. The system has no expensive or complicated components, yet the gasses are directly water cooled for its entire length once they leave the elbow off the manifold.

The exhaust system in the subject boat being but a year old, there was nothing to write up, not even a rusty hose clamp nor any dribble from a loose connection.

A cylindrical, transparent-walled strainer in the engine cooling-water intake line explained the absence of a scoop strainer over the through hull on the outside. I remarked that this seemed an expensive way to cut down the slight drag of a scoop strainer, but allowed that possibly the owner had had a bad experience with marine growth closing off an intake and had opted not to risk having to swim down with a screwdriver to clear the slots of an outside strainer. Provided that there is a seacock on the intake line, an in-line strainer can be removed for cleaning when it begins to clog, and the intake itself can be cleaned by briefly opening the cock and reaming the bore with a wire or screwdriver (some seacocks are provided with a Y for this purpose).

From the inside of the boat one could also see why the engine intake was the only through hull in the bottom of this particular boat. The galley sink drain connected through a Y valve to the diaphragm bilge pump, which discharged through a Delrin through hull in the transom, normally above the waterline and not provided with a seacock or valve. The cockpit drains were similarly fitted through the transom, and the toilet turned out to be a self-contained portable type. With these arrangements, not only a bit of drag but considerable money was saved. At the same time, I doubted that this young couple would long tolerate such spartan arrangements.

Most of the wiring on the boat was in harnesses, obviously made up specifically for this model by the builder. The battery power was controlled by a vaporproof master switch and a panel with circuit breakers. There were also a few toggle switches for electronic items that had their own fuses.

By way of working forward from the mechanical-plumbing-electrical department aft, it was time to pull up the hatches in the cabin sole. There, in the wafflelike reinforcement piece over the stub keel, was the diaphragm bilge pump's pickup hose. In this canoe-bodied craft the stub keel was certainly the low point, or sump, and the manufacturer had provided limber holes through the floor timber and stringer-like folds of this single-piece reinforcing laminate.

Remembering the cracks on the exterior along the joint between the lead keel and the stub keel, I examined the reinforcing member for any breaks, cracks, or signs of delamination from the hull in way of the stub keel. As far as I could discover there were no problems of any kind with the structure. The keel bolts were well buried under fiberglass in the bottom of the waffle pockets.

Forward in the bilge, I came upon the speedometer sensing unit, which consisted of a plastic cylinder with a paddle-wheel generator, made tight with 0 rings in a plastic through hull that was heavily bedded to the hull in silicone. Strangely, the cylinder, removable for clearing the paddle wheel, was lashed down in the through hull with nylon twine in lieu of a retaining pin, which ought to have been slipped through matching holes near the top of cylinder and through hull. The pin had not been lost; it was attached to the through hull with a length of chain. Not being blessed with microsecond logic, I had to study the situation to figure that one out. It seemed that the pin was used not only to secure the cylinder but to align it so that the paddle wheel would rotate in a fore-and-aft plane, but someone had installed the through hull so that its holes caused the wheel to head off to port about 10 degrees. Naturally, whoever had discovered the error had rotated the cylinder to the correct heading and lashed it down. I would recommend that a new hole be drilled in the cylinder to match the through hull's position; judging by the glob of silicone in which it was all but buried, disturbing the through hull could well be the end of it.

Farther forward, also on the centerline and again surrounded by a fat cushion of silicone, was the depthsounder's transducer. Fortunately, there was no alignment problem with the transducer's single through-the-hull part, but one could only imagine the problem or rash of problems befalling the manufacturer that could have caused all of this boat's through hulls to be swimming in silicone.

The mast step sat atop the central fore-and-aft stringer of the keel-reinforcing laminate. The metal step was about the same width as the stringer and was either lagged or bolted to it, but the top of the stringer was rounded, not dead flat, so that despite four fastenings, the step seemed perched unsteadily there. As I stared at it and wished that the sole could be taken up to perhaps disclose what the fastenings were, Marc volunteered that the builder was due to perform "some rework on that mast step." This was good news to me, since my instinctive reaction had been to doubt its stability under pressure, the most crucial quality of a mast step.

From that point on, there was nothing amiss with the boat worth discussing here. The rest of the details of the boat's construction, hardware, rig, and equipment were noted for inclusion in the report. After running through my checklist and reciting once more, for the benefit of the buyers, the few flaws that we had found, I left them preparing their "case" for further negotiations with the owner. As we parted, there was little doubt in any of our minds that the purchase of the boat would be completed, unless there was an adamant refusal on the part of the owner, the builder, or both to make some sort of adjustment for or repair of the one serious problem, the toerail and deck joint with the leaking pop rivets.

The report is reproduced herewith.

TO: Marc Kleinman

SURVEY OF: Auxiliary sloop

DIMENSIONS: 30' x 11'1" x 5'9"

REGISTRY:

HULL CONSTRUCTION: Fiberglass (single-skin) with balsa-cored raised deck (or flush deck). Stub keel with bolted-on lead fin.

EXTERIOR CONDITION: No serious scratches or dings, fair and smooth. No apparent repairs.

INTERIOR CONDITION: Clean and unmarred; clean bilges. Joinerwork shows little wear. Some small stains from deck rivets.

DECK CONDITION: Clean and unblemished except for silicone on toerails and one chainplate and cracks in cockpit sole gelcoat.

RUDDER: Sound. Has some stress cracks where tiller fits on, has small patch at lower pintle, needs two stop bolts in upper gudgeon.

PROPELLER: Bronze Martec, folding, RH, 13" x 8".

SHAFT: ¾" stainless.

STRUTS AND BEARINGS: Bronze strut, four-bolt; cutlass bearing. Bronze rubber-neck stuffing box, needs tightening or repacking.

ENGINE: BMW type D7 H061 15LB diesel, No. 581080001385. Not running, being winterized, but very clean and showing no external leaks or damage. Raw-water cooled.

EXHAUST: Water-cooled elbow to hose to water-lift muffler, to hose to transom.

FUEL TANK: 8 gal. cylindrical, mounted abaft engine under cockpit sole; aluminum, strapped down, all fittings in top.
    FILL: Hose through deck plate in cockpit sole.
    VENT: Hose to vent in transom.
    SUPPLY: Hose to filter, return hose, also.

BATTERY: Single 12-volt; not on board at survey.

WIRING: Mostly harness, rubber and thermoplastic-covered with protective sleeve over runs through boat.

FUSES AND SWITCHES: Toggle and circuit breaker. Vapor-proof master switch.

AUX. GENERATOR:

SHORE POWER:

VENTILATION: Forward hatch, companionway, aft-opening windows in transom.

STEERING SYSTEM: Tiller. Some wear in its bolt hole through rudderhead.

THROUGH HULLS: One bronze engine intake; three Delrin in transom for cockpit scuppers and bilge pump. Depthfinder and speedo, plastic.

SEACOCKS: One bronze on engine intake.

BILGE PUMP: Henderson diaphragm type mounted at after end of cockpit; exhausts through transom; teed to sink drain; pickup in stub keel.

STOVES & HEATERS:

REFRIGERATION: Igloo.

FIRE EXTINGUISHERS: Two Kiddie 10 BC, one by companionway, one on forepeak bulkhead, both read charged.

GROUND TACKLE: Danforth 20 H with circa 200 feet ⅜" nylon and short chain on anchor; galvanized.

SAFETY, LIFESAVING, AND TENDER: Bow pulpit and single lifelines; owner to install full aft pulpit and lower line. 5 CG-approved life jackets.

DECK HARDWARE: Stainless steel and aluminum. Two Lewmar #30 sheet winches; two #8 halyard winches; one spare.

ELECTRONICS AND NAVIGATION: Aquameter "Gemini" 4" spherical bulkhead-mount compass; Datamarine 100KL speedometer; Datamarine B 200 DL depthfinder; Ray Jefferson 1425 VHF/FM radio.

SPARS: Aluminum mast, boom, and spinnaker pole.

STANDING RIGGING: Stainless steel 1 x 19, swaged, with stainless steel turnbuckles.

RUNNING RIGGING: 7 x 19 stainless steel wire and braided, color-coded Dacron.

SAILS: Not surveyed, said to be like new.

WATER TANK: Two, one polyethylene and one plastic-bag type, Y-valved to sink pump, filled and vented internally, under starboard quarter berth.

COMMENTS: A very clean, like-new boat in all respects except as noted under the attached Recommendations and above. I found no signs of major previous damage or repairs.

If the attached Recommendations are acted upon, I would think that this boat is an outstanding example of its model line with top fair market value and insurability for its age of approximately one year.

RECOMMENDATIONS:

1) A heavy external application of silicone along the corners where the toerails meet the deck as well as stains on the interior indicate that the pop rivets fastening the rail through the deck edge and hull flange are weeping. It is recommended that the rivets be removed and replaced with flathead machine screws with nuts and washers on the interior. It would be best if the rails were taken up and rebedded in 3M 5200 or similar, but at least the bolts should be loaded with bedding, and there should be a ring of cotton under the washers. I consider replacement with bolts important for two other reasons: They will secure the toerails better, and they will provide a better mechanical backup attachment of the deck to the hull, which is now dependent mainly on whatever glue was used when the deck was installed, except where genoa tracks or other deck hardware bolts are located.

2) There are gelcoat stress cracks in the corner radius of the seat fronts to cockpit sole, indicating that the structure is a bit too flexible. It is hard to say whether, or how soon, the fiberglass might crack through. A neatly applied additional angle of laminate in the corner would be most effective, but for now, the corner could be sanded and regelcoated, or painted, and watched for reappearance of the cracks. It seems to be the seat fronts that are too thin, so some additional fiberglass applied to them on the interior, overlapping the bottom corner, would be most effective.

3) The speedometer through hull is headed off the centerline of the boat, but seems solid, so I suspect that it was installed that way. A new retaining pin hole in the sensor housing aligned with the one in the through hull will allow it to be pinned down when headed forward.

4) For cruising, a scoop strainer will help to prevent clogging of the engine saltwater intake between the hull and the internal strainer.

5) The tiller bolt is wearing a bit loose in the rudderhead. It should

be kept fairly tight, and a cotter pin installed if it tends to work loose. But the hole can always be filled and rebored, or sleeved. I would use Marine-Tex if I filled it.

6) It was said that the mast step is to be reworked on warranty. I would like to see that done, as I do not think the step has a good bearing on the rounded top of the fiberglass member. Because the sole is screwed down, I also could not tell whether the fastenings of the step to the fiberglass were bolts or lags. The latter might be all right if the step had a flatter bearing surface, but I would want these to be bolts given the surface that it's on.

NOTE: My qualifications for this survey are over 40 years of boatbuilding in wood and fiberglass, with more than 200 boats built in my custom boatshop, plus repairs and surveys. The above are my considered opinions, without prejudice. I cannot be responsible for mistakes in judgment, omissions, or undetected defects. This survey does not contain a complete inventory.

4

Boat Pox

The prospective buyer of the 35-foot sloop was a college professor and neighbor for whom I had already done two surveys. His unusual request that I survey the boat in the water made sense. The sailing season was over, and a decision to buy or not buy would determine whether she would be hauled in his yard or the owner's. "A survey in the water would save one move either way," he said, "unless it turned out after the boat was brought to my place that it had a very bad defect only discernable below the waterline on the outside."

"Right," I said, "and defects fitting that description are certainly unlikely." I didn't know then how unprophetic those words were.

The boat surveyed well enough in the water. She had had some repair to the topside gelcoat along the centerline joint, which nevertheless looked sound; she needed a new mast collar and boot; she showed some of the usual slight deck leaks; and she had one "frozen" seacock and a broken piece or two of hardware. All of these faults were acceptable to the buyer, who gave word to place the boat in his yard for winter storage.

Soon after the boat was taken there, I dropped by to check out the underwater parts. Her keel, shaft, strut, and propeller all passed inspection, but the rudder had been hit hard. I saw that it would need repairs to breaks in the fiberglass at the bottom forward corner and at the top around the stock. Neither its operation nor its attachment to the stock, however, seemed to have been impaired. Despite this newly discovered fault, the total estimated cost of repairs was, in the buyer's opinion, too small to justify renegotiating the price. The survey was wrapped up and the sale of the boat went forward.

A week or two later, the buyer called me, saying, "Would you mind stopping by and looking at these bumps on the bottom of the boat?"

"I'll come over now." I remembered the two or three lumps on the bottom, which had puzzled me when we first noticed them. I had theorized that these were probably "gelcoat blisters," which are caused by moisture trapped under gelcoat at the time it is applied. When the moisture is heated by the sun, it raises a bubble of the gelcoat.

When I arrived, the buyer pointed out that these blisters had grown in size. Further, although neither of us was sure, there seemed to be more of them than we had noticed when she was first hauled out.

This time we actually broke open some blisters, using a small screwdriver and hammer to chip away the gelcoat. When punctured, water ran out, and sure enough, the shell of the blisters was mostly gelcoat with only a slight involvement of chopped strands from the first layer of mat beneath it. The rest of the laminate behind the blisters was quite solid and absolutely unaffected as far as we could tell.

"Well," I said, "at least it's a surface condition and doesn't affect the integrity of the structure. Luckily, the bumps are all below the waterline, although why that should be, I don't know. The vast majority of blisters I have seen, caused by moisture under the gelcoat, have appeared *above* the waterline, yet there's no sign that these topsides have ever had a single blister. The other fact that bothers me is that they should still be coming out on a 10-year-old boat. This can't be the first time the sun has heated her underwater surfaces, especially since she has spent some years in Florida. I guess if she were my boat, I'd just grind off the bumps and fill the craters with a putty—one made of gelcoat stiffened with talc, a proprietary putty like one of the polyester autobody putties, or an epoxy-based putty like Marine-Tex."

The professor agreed, and that appeared to be the end of it; we went our separate ways through the winter. In midspring, however, he called to bring me up to date on a situation to which I had previously had but a passing introduction. Not only had more blisters appeared, but while grinding away bottom paint around them the professor had discovered patches of putty, which were obviously filling the craters of old blisters similar to the current crop. Thus alerted, he had removed more bottom paint and had discovered that the whole bottom was peppered with previously repaired blisters.

Like a true scholar the professor had researched this matter, and he handed me copies of several papers and magazine articles discussing a fiberglass boat skin disease that, while very rare in northern climates, afflicts a small but consistent percentage of boats kept in southern waters.

The consensus of the reports was that, given a porous gelcoat and warm water, water will penetrate the gelcoat and set up a reaction with the resin of the layer beneath. More and more water is drawn in by osmosis to combine with the liquid solution thus formed; pressure mounts, and a blister of gelcoat is raised. Added heat, such as that from the sun shining on the hauled-out hull, can quicken the blisters' growth by causing gas or vapor formation, but the blisters are essentially liquid. When you break them, the liquid smells similar to uncured resin.

The reports also agreed that an unusually porous gelcoat is a prerequisite of this boat pox, but relatively warm water seems to be more or less essential, too. Conflicting estimates and numbers aside, the problem is well known in Florida and hardly known at all in New England. Boat pox may, too, occur more readily or rapidly in fresh water than salt water, due both to the warm summer temperature and the low osmotic concentrations of freshwater bodies.

Prevention is a matter of quality control when the boat is manufactured, ensuring that the gelcoat is not porous. Almost as obvious are the recommended treatments: The least expensive approach is to grind off individual blisters, allow them to dry, and then fill and seal them. If the blistering is too widespread or rapid to contain in this fashion, one must take off all the gelcoat below the waterline and replace it with a nonporous coating. A minimum of two coats of an epoxy paint seems to be the best existing sealant, having a low porosity and adhering very well to the laminate.

"I had the gelcoat sandblasted off," said the professor. "If you want to look at her, she's still at the yard, waiting until I get some prices for painting her with epoxy and, of course, applying new bottom paint. Meanwhile, I'm talking with the people who sold her to me, and I'd like you to write a report on the whole blister business that I can submit to them."

One of the endearing things about being a surveyor is being right in the middle of any trouble, but lest you suspect that a law suit was in the offing, I should mention that the boat was one of those given to a school by an owner whose tax bracket makes a charitable gift less unprofitable than selling his boat. Thus it was understandable that the most recent previous owner, the school, was unaware of the condition of her underbody. Unfortunately, if, as the surveyor, I had had more experience with this type of problem and had recognized it right away, I might have spared all parties to the sale considerable embarrassment, myself most of all. The moral of the story is that a surveyor can never learn enough about boats and their potential problems.

The usually-but-not-always-permanent cure for a case of boat pox—grinding away the gelcoat and refinishing the surface with epoxy paint—is not cheap. At today's boatyard prices, I estimate the *minimum* cost to range from about $2,000 for a 25-footer to $8,000 for a 40-footer. An important question far from resolution at this writing is who shall pay for the cure. To this point, the reactions of manufacturers have run the gamut from doing the repair or paying for it long after the warranty has run out, to an adamant denial of any responsibility even though the boat is still under warranty because it's a "cosmetic problem, and these are not covered under warranty." Recently there has been a loud outcry over what seem to be the "one in a million" cases in which the pox, by wicking along unsaturated glass strands, escapes the confines of its usual locus at the interface of gelcoat and first underlying layer of glass reinforcement, migrates into the deeper layers of the laminate, and there finds uncured resin on which to "feed." In such an instance the boat can be devoured from within. Because of the furor, the Coast Guard is showing interest for the first time in studying boat pox as something that can reach the status of a structural defect. They have refused to investigate the disease in the past, considering it rare and not in any way dangerous to recreational boaters. And that it isn't, usually.

5

The Mislaid Deck

She was a pretty little 31-foot double-ended wooden auxiliary cutter, custom built to the plans of a well-known designer except for some changes in rig, layout, and construction details made by the owner and the builder. As the lift raised her from her element onto the tarmac for our survey, her flowing lines, the rightness of their Tancook Whaler heritage, and the art of the designer who had remolded them as a small yacht hushed our chattering. "Lovely boat!" said the broker softly, as though he did not wish to embarrass her.

"Look at that shape! He was some designer!" I murmured, destroying my air of professional neutrality.

"Amen!" said the prospective buyer.

Her hull of traditional cedar planking on an oak frame was in sound condition, as certainly it should be at a mere five years of age. Her rig and sails were good; her interior, trimmed in blond oak, was charming and in excellent condition; and she had a sturdy little two-cylinder diesel engine. The prospective buyer and I were doing just fine with the survey until we started to investigate some curled-up ends of the bare iroko decking.

Here and there about the deck, the end of a stave was projecting as much as ¼ to ⅜ inch above its neighbors, stretching the Thiokol seam compound upward with it. Dampness beneath and drying on top were obviously causing the curling, and I reasoned that moisture must be gaining access under the stave ends. Either the only fastenings in the decking were over the deck beams—and there were none between the beams and none specifically in the butted stave ends, most of which fell between the beams—or the Thiokol, ordinarily an excellent glue, was not anchoring these ends tightly to the subdecking and bedding them against the intrusion of moisture as it should.

Checking the underside of the deck, I found that the iroko was laid over plywood. Some measurements from a portlight in the trunk side to the top and bottom of the deck told me that its total thickness was about ¾ inch, allowing approximately ⅜ inch each for the plywood and the decking. While looking I thought I might find some "backing screws" up through the plywood into the decking, such as boatbuilders used years ago in double planking before any glue was considered waterproof. Close examination of the overhead turned up nothing of the kind. There was, however, a ripple in the surface of the overhead under both side decks. "That has to be delamination of the plywood," I said, and the prospective buyer agreed. Rapping on the plywood's undersurface and probing it with an ice pick, we found that the plywood was not only delaminated but soft with rot in much of the area in way of the cabin trunk, and very soft in a smaller area that corresponded with the outline of puddles that had been forming on each side amidships, near the low point of the sheer. Dry as the day was, both exterior stains and interior rot told us that the starboard damage was larger in area than that to port. "Why do you suppose that is?" asked the prospective buyer.

"Perhaps because of the list to starboard. I noticed that the marine growth comes up an inch or so over the boottop to starboard but falls short of it to port."

"I would want to move some ballast and take that out of her."

"So would I. At the same time, puddles of any kind on deck are not normal, and they should be avoided on any boat, no matter what the material under this is. Not only should her fore-and-aft trim be checked when she is afloat to be certain that the last trickle of deck

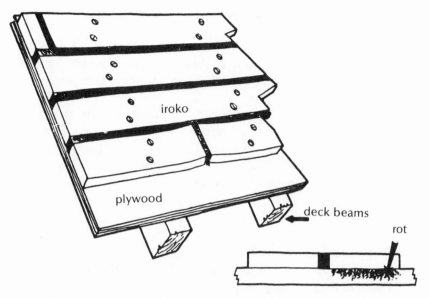

The iroko decking of the 31-foot double-ender was not bedded in seam compound, and there were no fastenings at butts that fell between deck beams. As a result, moisture had attacked the plywood subdeck and was causing the stave ends to curl. In short, a scarcely believable building oversight that would cost $10,000 or more to repair.

water finds its way out through a scupper, but the owner should also make sure that those who haul her out for 'dry' storage don't leave her bow down, as is often done."

"I know. I've seen some small ponds on boats in winter storage. From the looks, this boat's side decks have been wet more than dry."

The side deck problem was a discouraging letdown, but the plywood was firm for some inches outboard of the trunk sides. "Well," I ventured, "it does look as though the side decks can be rebuilt without taking the trunk off. Only the toerail and some hardware would have to come up. Now let's have a good look at the rest of the deck to see what other problems there might be."

"I think we had better do that," replied the prospective buyer, visibly depressed.

From forward of the trunk all the way to the bow, the plywood had a healthy, solid sound when rapped from below with a screwdriver handle.

"The foredeck might have some random soft spots," I allowed, "but what we have tapped and probed looks, sounds, and feels all right from this side. We can study it further when we go on deck."

Moving aft to study the underside of the deck abaft the cabin trunk, I felt something soft up against the bridge deck. "Feels as though there's insulation in these two bays over the engine," I announced, reaching back for the flashlight. But there wasn't. It was the plywood I had touched, soft and puffy as a bed pillow with rot!

"Good Lord! This whole bridge deck is gone," I exclaimed. "Just look at this!"

We decided, after probing and rapping, that the condition extended just outboard of the coamings on both sides.

"Too bad the coamings are involved," I said, "but they're edge-bolted through the deck and screwed to the fairing blocks on the trunk sides, so they'll come up fairly easily. Unfortunately, the plywood layer of the deck extends forward under the after endpiece of the trunk, so it would be a bit tricky to repair this without lifting the trunk. Still, with luck, one might clean the old plywood out and wedge a new piece in there, slotting it for the through bolts that run edgewise down through the trunk sides into the carlings."

The prospective buyer looked glum as he summed up our findings on the deck's condition: "That's both side decks, approximately through the length of the cabin trunk, and the whole bridge deck out into the side decks that need replacement so far."

"Yes," I said, "and then there are those lifted ends of the iroko scattered all over the deck. Those that are not in an area that is taken up anyway are going to need some sort of treatment, so we should go on deck and have another look at them."

Selecting one of the most curled-up staves on the deck aft, we sliced open the seam Thiokol across its end, pried it up clear of the adjoining staves, and peeked into the "mouth" we had opened. As far as I could see, there was no evidence of glue or bedding compound of any kind in the interface between stave and plywood. "Look at that!" I said. "There's no bedding or glue under this stave. The Thiokol is only in the seams!"

The prospective buyer looked, then took the ice pick and probed under the end, sliding it right through the plywood as easily as through a piece of cheese. "Rotten!" he announced.

"Yes, and no wonder," I replied. "The staves aren't fastened down except at deck beams, and they weren't glued with anything that I can see except what little Thiokol crept in under their edges. I can hardly believe it, but I think the staves were simply laid down on bare plywood and screwed at the deck beams with spacers between them, then the Thiokol was applied to the seams. Certainly, if there was some sort of glue or bedding material used, it didn't hold the staves down or keep the water out from under them. I'm afraid we have to say that the whole deck is on its way to join the side decks and bridge deck, and incredible as it may seem on a five-year-old boat, the entire deck ought to be taken up and replaced. To do it right, that means taking off everything, right down to the deck beams."

"I'm afraid you're right," said the prospective buyer. "So what should we do now?"

"Well, as the prospective buyer you have three options that I know of. You can turn down the boat, you could get some estimates for a new deck and renegotiate with the owner, or you could let the broker transmit the bad news to the owner and see whether he offers to have the deck rebuilt. Meanwhile, my job is to write up the survey so that you will have all of our findings on record, whatever happens."

The prospective buyer went to discuss the matter with the broker, and I heard no more about the boat until I talked with the broker several weeks later.

"What happened to the pretty little double-ender?" I asked.

"Nuthin'. The estimates to replace the deck ranged from $9,500 to $15,000. The owner wouldn't lower his price enough, and the negotiations broke down. She's still sitting right there, but that's his problem now, not mine."

No doubt the depressing discovery of the rotting deck was too much of a shock for the owner, who had been asking $30,000, had agreed to take $25,000 subject to survey, but was now faced with getting no more than half his asking price. "Too bad," I said. "Pretty little boat!"

"Right!" he agreed. "Lovely boat."

6

The Moribund Ones

While it is still hard to say under just what circumstances most fiberglass boats will meet their end, we know for sure that wooden boats all become feeble or sick and must die sooner or later, except in museums. It is inevitable that a surveyor will occasionally find himself gloomily assessing the problems of one that is terminally ill. When there is little or no hope of recovery, when deterioration is so far advanced that an attempt to reverse it would be financially disastrous, then it becomes the surveyor's unpleasant duty to lay out the facts pointing to that conclusion.

If not glossed over, these facts are almost certain to dissuade the prospective buyer, dash the owner's hope of unloading his burden for cash, and wipe out the broker's fee. It is a turn of events not likely to increase the surveyor's popularity with the latter two persons, at least in the short term. If he wishes, however, to enjoy long-term respect in his trade, he must report the boat's condition—not sensationally or didactically, but accurately no matter how sad— and he must recommend whatever treatment he considers necessary, no matter how drastic. If he must say that she should be broken up or that her value should be reduced to salvage only, then he must. That's the job, and there is no other way to do it.

"Why?" I sometimes ask myself, when the usually not unpleasant study of a hull and deck has turned into a dismal catalog of disrepair and rampant rot. "Why am I being paid to report that this boat is an absolute ruin? It's so obvious!"

Despite my lament, not everyone has the experience to understand the implications of a boat's problems in terms of the weakened structure, the nature and amount of repair or rebuilding called for, or the expense involved.

While mortal sickness is not always the reason for it, a low price should at least arouse one's suspicion that a boat is nearing the end of her useful life, and a low, low price could well mean that she has reached it. A young friend sent me to Connecticut to survey a stock wooden powerboat with a stunningly low price. He could see that she was old and tired; what he needed to know was whether it was practicable to rebuild her, for she was just the sort of "nice, classic, wooden motorboat" he would like to get and "fix up." Unfortunately, I found dozens of broken ribs, a number of planks that were loose because of those breaks and a needed refastening, and mahogany plywood bulkheads that had been eaten back by rot an average of about 3 inches from the hull. Draped over her keel blocking and cradle arms like a bag of cement, she looked too weak to survive a trip over the road to my young friend's yard without carefully arranged extra support. It was not, however, the problem of moving her so much as the estimated cost of restoring so many ailing parts that was building up doubt about the advisability of the purchase. Already, less than an hour into the survey, she appeared to be a poor investment. Still, rather than come to a hasty conclusion, I decided to look around on deck; if she was all right there, I would continue with an investigation of her mechanical systems, gear, and equipment.

It took less than a half hour to locate rot in the guardrails, toerails, pilothouse sides, and windshield, and, where its fiberglass cloth covering had split, in the softwood "streamlined" curves of the cabin trunk. Most of these were not small rot pockets but extensive soft-as-cheese areas that would require major surgery. Seeing all this was the last straw. I aborted the survey and headed for home with the sad news that properly restoring this boat could cost as much as building a new one like her. The forlorn craft obviously hadn't moved from her resting place for several years, and I doubt she will until it is time to go to the dump. But if somebody does try to revive her, my heart goes out to that person, for it will be a task of heroic proportions.

The next boat my young friend sent me to survey had a higher price tag, and sure enough, she looked more the way a twin-screw stock boat should look when I spotted her in an outside winter storage lineup. She was well painted, her shape was not noticeably hogged, and she had all the signs of recent use rather than of neglected repose in a boatyard. Walking around her, I saw that her planking was smooth and fair, the seams even and close. Her propellers, shafts, and rudders were in good condition. The strut and intermediate bearings had no play. For once on a stock boat of this type and age, the plank-on-edge keel was not tilted to one side, and even the garboard seams looked reasonably tight. I was just about satisfied that the bottom was in fine shape for the boat's age, and I was taking a last look over it when my eye caught the sketchy outlines through thick bottom paint of five fastening bungs across one plank at one rib. "Oh, NO!" I thought. "They haven't done THAT."

But, as I studied the surface from different angles until a grazing light accentuated the faint impressions of the bungs, it soon became evident that someone had, indeed, added fastenings to the entire bottom.

To install new fastenings *between* the old and not in their place is storing up future trouble. It only postpones the day of reckoning, when the wasted old fastenings must be removed and their holes plugged against leaking. It also perforates the planks with closely spaced holes; weakens the ribs with added holes, too; and leaves each plank-to-rib joint with but two effective fastenings where there were three, or one where there were two. As if this were not enough, many boats have suffered hollowed-out ribs where water seeping in along old and wasted fastenings has trickled down the outboard faces of the ribs and rotted grooves in them. The hollow ribs, which look sound enough on their three visible sides, will often escape suspicion until planks loosen and an attempt to replace fastenings finds no firm material until the drill pops through the thin shell of the rib's inboard face.

As far as this survey was concerned, the refastening job was

When the paint is broken along the plank seams (**above**), *you can bet the fastenings are letting go. One look below the spray rail on the same boat* (**below**) *confirms it.*

"strike one." I was going to have to state that the hull could no longer be trusted while those old fastenings were wasting away in the planking, and that she had been significantly, permanently weakened by so many additional fastening holes. My recommendation would be that the most practical and economically viable way to return this hull to full strength and flawless watertight integrity would be to cover it with fiberglass, at least to the waterline. Having covered dozens of hulls that were all but hopelessly feeble, and having written a book that has helped many other repairers to cover boats successfully by the same method, I am quite confident that it works.*

A cold-molded wooden skin, in which two or more layers of thin planking are set in a waterproof glue such as resorcinol or epoxy, is another solution for a boat in this condition. Applying this skin is equivalent to building a one-piece shell in place on each side of the hull. Cold-molded construction is stronger for its weight than traditional plank-on-frame methods, and, being seamless, is relatively maintenance-free for long periods. When laid up over old carvel planking with at least two crossing diagonal layers, it returns watertight integrity and almost exactly the kinds of strength and stiffness to a tired hull that the years have stolen. Having restored a number of boats by applying cold-molded planking, I know that it works just fine as long as the keel area of the boat is sound enough to connect the resultant half shells. If the boat is too far gone along the centerline to be strengthened economically with wood, it may be necessary to build up fiberglass around the keel and out onto the deadrise, so that the cold-molded planking coming to the keel laps over it for a foot or two.

Both cold-molded and fiberglass coverings are far less expensive than rebuilding the original plank-on-frame hull (or deck). A fiberglass covering is much less expensive than cold molding, although, all other things being equal, a cold-molded covering should add a bit more to the resale value of the boat. Fiberglass has several additional advantages: It is suitable for lapstrake boats,

---

*The book is Covering Wooden Boats with Fiberglass, *International Marine Publishing Company, 1981.*

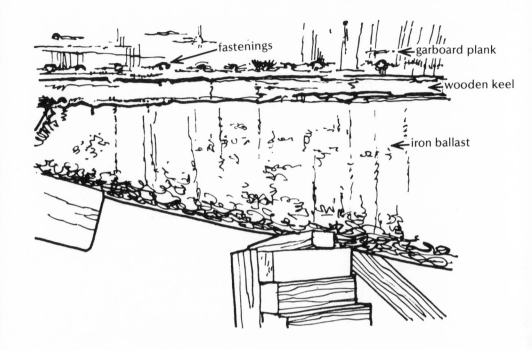

The subject of this sketch is an elderly wooden sailboat in her cradle. Her iron keel, wooden keel timber, and garboard plank all seem intent on parting company. The garboard's lower edge has had more than enough additional fastenings, which have significantly weakened the garboard without pulling the parts together. Most probably the keelbolts are wasted, and should be replaced, but has the wooden keel been softened by rot? If it has, the best hope might be to cover the bottom with fiberglass that would completely encase the iron ballast. If it hasn't, perhaps it will be enough to replace the garboard fastenings (or possibly the garboard), leaving no wasted fastening holes to cause further trouble. More likely nothing will be done, and this boat will soon be a moribund one.

easily applied to any shape, and can be thickened locally to overcome such weaknesses as a row of broken ribs, loosened backbone members, or wasted keel bolts. Moreover, a fiberglass covering is even more maintenance-free than a cold-molded skin. All things considered, then, a cold-molded covering is only for those who want to avoid putting fiberglass on their boats.

On the other hand, covering a boat with fiberglass is not cheap, and an owner should weigh its cost against the projected resale value of the boat.

A bit shaken by the realization that I had come close to missing the added fastenings in the bottom, I now proceeded to study the topsides with great care. They had recently been well painted, "to sell the boat," I thought to myself. "Well, it's fair enough to put on a good appearance. I'll just have to look more sharply for signs of trouble."

I had hardly told myself that when I discovered a spot on the stem with a faintly blistered look. When pressed with my finger, it oozed a drop of moisture. Tapping with the plastic handle of the small screwdriver I like to carry, I heard a definitely softer sound, and this extended along the rabbet from the deck level halfway down to the waterline. Involved, too, were a number of hood ends of the planking. This was on the starboard side, but there was some to port as well. Naturally, I was itchy to try for depth, and despite the smooth paint job I managed to find a few places along the rabbet line and plank seams as well as in the slit in the blister I had broken where my ice pick could enter, yet the paint or putty could be made to cover the hole afterward. There was little resistance to sliding the ice pick into the wood a couple of inches.

"Hah! You sneaky rascals," I muttered to whomever was responsible. "We'll have to have an extra close look at every rot-prone spot in this bucket, seeing that you like to hide them under paint and putty."

Sure enough, there was a softness in the forward corners of the trunk and the pilothouse that required stubborn suspicion to find and careful thumping and probing to verify without disrupting the glossy finish. On the inside, dampness indicated leaking joints opposite these spots, but the softness on the outside had not yet worked all the way through the wood. The interior, however, had its

*The forward lower corner of a windshield is a classic location
of incipient rot.*

own problems. While checking out the cabin trunk corners for leaks,
some wetness in a dinette cushion directed my attention to the
window in the trunk side above it. The wood below that window,
which was covered by a heavy drape, was all but rotted away for
several inches where water had worked down the trunk side from
under the glass, and the mahogany was softer than balsa wood for
most of its one-inch thickness. Only a very thin layer of wood on the
outside was stiff enough to hold the paint and to make a bond with
the putty or glazing compound that covered the edges of the glass.
"Almost fooled again!" I winced at the thought of my embarrassment if I had not lifted the drapes, or if I had not felt the wetness in
the dinette cushion that led me to look at the windows (both sides of
the trunk had identical problems). But I was angered, too, that I had
not discovered these two areas in my inspection of the exterior, for

vigorous enough tapping would have signaled the difference between an inch of solid wood and a fraction of an inch of it over rot.

After checking out the other aspects of the boat, I packed up and started for home, dropping off the keys at the office of the boatyard owner, who also happened to be brokering the boat. "How did she look?" he asked.

"Well, she has plenty of problems," I allowed. "Otherwise, pretty good."

"Problems? Gee, that's funny," he said. "She's been going good, going real good right up to last fall."

"Could have, I suppose. Thanks, I'll see you."

The report I prepared for my young friend said, among other, less important things:

1) Either all of the original bottom fastenings must be removed and the holes filled with new fastenings or wooden plugs, or the bottom, if not the whole hull, should be covered with thick, mechanically fastened fiberglass.

2) A large section of the stem and the forward ends of a number of the planks must be replaced; alternatively, if the hull were covered with fiberglass, dutchmen could be cut into the soft areas and these areas could be saturated with preservative and covered with a heavy laminate to return full strength to the structure.

3) Sections of the forward faces and corners of the trunk and pilothouse must be replaced.

4) Sections of the trunk sides under the side windows or deadlights must be replaced.

5) The purchase of this boat should not be closed until the buyer has satisfactory estimates in hand for the above work, and, if possible, some adjustment in the purchase price to help cover its cost. That is to say, before closing the purchase, the purchaser needs to know what the total cost of returning the boat to a viable condition will be.

Sadly, before my young friend could get estimates together—due to builders and repairers being busy with their spring work—the

A moribund one. Think you can save her? Possibly, but it will cost you. Once a boat has been opened up by the weather as this one has been, she cannot last much longer.

time period for which his deposit held the boat ran out and he was forced to turn her down. Probably that was the wisest course, since the total cost of restoring the boat to good health was still an unknown. I don't know where she is today. She may have been made whole again. If so, it must have taken a substantial amount of time or money or both. I believe it more likely, however, that someone bought her not knowing much about her ailments, that only the most obvious flaws were repaired, and that she has continued to slip into worse condition. If so, having had but a marginal chance of survival several years ago, she must now have passed the point where rebuilding would be economically worthwhile, and one of these days she'll be found sitting out in the back corner of some lot, abandoned and moribund.

A typical survey of a boat hovering on the edge of extinction is reprinted below. Without much reading between the lines one should be able to tell that rot is raging over the boat's exterior. It has also infected the garboard area on the inside. She needs refastening, she is beginning to hog, her twin engines and propellers are mismatched, and her wiring, piping, and gas bottle installation are dangerous. Not specifically detailed is the "rebuilding" of her interior with thin, discount-store plywood (made for interior "home improvements") fastened with finish nails and extensively covered with carpeting. The use of such materials is bound to slash the value of any traditionally built wooden boat. More intolerable from the viewpoint of safety and keeping the hull "sweet" is the fact that this interior work was installed without providing access to the rudder stuffing boxes, steering mechanism, strut bolts, exhaust outlets, fuel tanks and their connections, or any number of other items and areas that need surveillance, maintenance, and ready accessibility in an emergency. Further, no air strakes or holes have been left to ventilate the hull structure, and this has created a condition very likely to accelerate the spread of rot.

When we went to survey this boat, she had been standing for several years between two houses in a thickly settled part of town, under tall trees, without a weather cover. Like many an ailing boat laid up ashore until her owner could get around to repairing her, she had been sitting there unattended for too long. Exposed to the dank atmosphere under those trees—the shadows and the drip of fresh water—but denied the counteracting effects of brilliant sun and drying winds, she had grown ever more sodden as area after area succumbed to creeping decay. "Depressing, isn't it?" I commented to the man who did the survey with me, speaking softly as if out of respect for a terminally ill person.

"It's a shame!" he muttered. "She's so far gone."

"If they don't move her soon, they'll need a dump truck, not a trailer. Let's go home and write up the bad news."

SURVEY OF: A 42' twin screw motor yacht, built in 1955.

CONSTRUCTION: Oak and mahogany frame; cedar planking, double on bottom, seam batten on topsides; plywood and fiberglass-covered forward deck and housetops; copper-rivet and bronze-screw fastened. Interior remodeled, see Recommendations.

HULL CONDITION: Some areas fair, some poor, some bad. See Recommendations.

DECK CONDITION: Same as hull. See Recommendations.

INTERIOR CONDITION: Interior of hull construction obscured from view by remodeling of arrangement. Remodeling not done yacht fashion. See Recommendations.

UNDERWATER GEAR: 1¼" bronze shafts; bronze, flax-packed intermediate struts; bronze struts with rubber bearings. Both bearing inserts need replacement.

Port propeller is 18" x 22" 3-blade, bronze; starboard propeller is 16" x 15" 4-blade, bronze, loose on shaft.

Stuffing boxes are rubber neck, cast bronze, bolted to a backing block on the planking. Fastenings have been added; many are suspect, and the outboard edges of the blocks are soft. See Recommendations.

RUDDERS: Cast bronze spade. Inboard end of stocks, stuffing boxes, or rudder ports not accessible through interior arrangement.

STEERING SYSTEM: Hydraulic with wooden wheel at single station on fly bridge; ram at rudders not accessible for inspection. Lines are copper tubing.

ENGINES: Port engine is a Barr conversion, V-8 gasoline. Starboard engine is an OMC V-8 gasoline, model and serial numbers not decipherable. Owner was to demonstrate engines to buyer.

EXHAUST: Steam hose and stainless steel sections off water-cooled elbows on engines to transom. Transom end inboard not accessible.

FUEL TANKS: Look like Monel, but are at least stainless. Part of one only can be seen by removing drawers in port locker aft by transom. Everything else inaccessible, except fills extend through locker to deck plates in aft corners of aft cabintop. How the vent and supply lines are connected, or whether there are valves (which couldn't be reached anyway) cannot be studied. The fill deck plates did not seem to be grounded to the tank across the fill hoses.

ELECTRICAL: There was one battery on the platform forward of the engines at the time of the survey. No arrangement for securing and protecting the batteries was apparent. There was a vapor-proof master switch. The wiring in general was disorganized.

INSTRUMENTATION: Tachometer, water temperature, oil pressure, and ammeter for each engine at fly bridge.

ELECTRONICS AND NAVIGATION: 3½" Ritchie compass. Ray Jeff fathometer (not tested); transducer backing block for this at hull is soft.

THROUGH HULLS AND SEACOCKS: Head inlet has a gate valve which was too stiff to turn by hand. Head outlet seacock cannot be reached from the only opening hatch nearby. Head sink has no valve or seacock, needs three hose clamps. Head outlet hose clamp at seacock badly rusted.

Galley sink discharge is apparently pumped overboard by bilge pump. Wiring of this pump has open, twisted connections of bare wire.

There are abandoned through hulls flanking the engines that should be kept capped, plugged, or removed.

The aft head has no through hull connections, but the sink has one without seacock, and its hose needs clamps.

STOVE: 3-burner with oven. LPG gas bottle for it is stored under sink locker beside it. Very illegal and extremely dangerous.

REFRIGERATOR: Household type.

SHORE POWER: Receptacles seen on board, power cord not sighted.

HOT WATER HEATER: Electric, under sink counter.

GROUND TACKLE: A small Danforth-type anchor and a nylon rode sighted on board.

CONCLUSIONS: I do not believe that, in her present state, this boat is insurable. Neither do I believe she should be launched or used until extensive repairs to the defects pointed out above and in the following Recommendations are made.

It is very difficult to estimate the cost of correcting the many faults, but I would think a MINIMUM expenditure to make the boat seaworthy and insurable would be 15,000 dollars, and I hasten to add that many times that could be spent without bringing this boat to better than proper condition.

At the present time, then, I would place her value at salvage, whatever that may be.

RECOMMENDATIONS: It is recommended that the following list of deteriorated parts and defective conditions be corrected:

1) The exterior above the waterline is soggy from repeated incursions of fresh water, and a number of important parts—covering board, sheerstrake, cabin sides, corner posts, stem, and transom—will have to be pieced out or replaced, depending on their softness from rot as determined when they are stripped down, prodded, or otherwise exposed. That there are extensive areas which must be replaced can be easily demonstrated on the outside; but whether the whole stem or the whole transom, for instance, needs work, or how long a section of a given plank needs replacement, cannot be ascertained positively without stripping paint or at least studying the part on the inside. But the inside is sealed up very tightly in most places by the remodeling, without openings to allow inspection. No doubt, closing up so much of the inside of the hull with plywood and rugs has accelerated the rotting.

2) The bottom of the boat, too, has a large number of soft planking butts and hood ends, and over a large section of the garboard area the inner, diagonal planking is separated from the outer planking and is so soft that water squeezes out of it when it is pressed down. In this area the lower foot or so of the intermediate ribs is up off the bottom due to fastenings having given out.

3) Many of the bronze screws in the hull have wasted away completely, although those copper rivets we bared on the exterior were in fair shape. At any rate, there is a lot of refastening to be done.

4) The two shafts rest in the bottom of the shaft logs, and sighting the hull indicates that the stern has fallen considerably, a fact to which double stands at the stern also attest. The bottom of the aft end of the keel has a twist to port.

5) The fiberglass on the forward deck was merely turned up against the toerail and the cabin sides and front, allowing water to get behind it and start rot along these areas.

6) The bottom outer plank of the transom is broken in four places.

7) Some of the windows are bound to leak unless repaired.

8) The LPG bottle must be removed from the interior and installed elsewhere. The gasoline tanks should have shutoffs at the tank. The

stern must be opened up so that there is access to inspect and service the rudders and steering.

9) The piping and wiring should be reworked with an eye to safety.

NOTE: My qualifications for this survey are over 40 years of boatbuilding, including my own custom shop where more than 200 boats from 8 to 65 feet were built in wood and fiberglass. The above are my considered opinions, given without prejudice. I cannot be responsible for errors, omissions, or mistakes in judgment, and acceptance of this survey constitutes acceptance of that condition. This survey does not contain a complete inventory.

7

Imported Boats

While I happen to believe that more of the best yachts in the world have been designed and built within a hundred miles of where I live (Mattapoisett, Massachusetts) than in any other one area, I am also a firm believer in free trade. If better boats for the money can be built in other countries, Americans should be able to buy them. To make it otherwise would be to shake down our yachting countrymen for the difference in price and hand the money to American boatbuilders, and I cannot see that the yachtsmen of this country owe us boatbuilders a living. If we can't keep our share of the market by building better boats, we should try a different occupation. So far, however, judging by the imports that I have surveyed, I don't think we are an endangered species. In this chapter, I'll describe a few of the flaws found in imports.

The editors wanted to eliminate this chapter, feeling that its usefulness was impaired because I have not named names. But I don't think a book on surveying boats in this country would be complete if it failed to mention the flaws peculiar to some of the thousands upon thousands of imports that have joined our yachting fleet since World War II. Did I say some? The truth is, I have yet to survey one of these imports in its twelfth year or beyond without finding at least one problem that was both serious and, with a bit more care in the construction, entirely avoidable. There are two reasons why I have not named names, the first being that the boats when I survey them are usually at least several years old, and the problems I find may have been corrected in more recent years. Second, while I have surveyed many imports, I haven't seen them all by any means. It would be unfair to pick on those with which I happen to be familiar. Nevertheless, people who have owned, repaired, or surveyed one or more of the imports in my experience will recognize them in this chapter by their frailties. What follows will, I hope, serve as both a useful warning and a checklist of common trouble spots for anyone considering the purchase of *any* foreign import.

Let me identify precisely what I mean by an imported boat. From the surveyor's point of view, three kinds of foreign-built boats arrive in this country: those that are built for a foreign country's domestic market, but which happen to migrate here; those built in another country by order and to the plans or specifications of an American owner; and those produced in another country specifically for export to the United States.

I have found the boats indigenous to other developed countries to be good, although differently built; some of them are just about perfect. I have also seen some boats, though by no means all, constructed in other countries under the supervision of the American owner or his agent that were beautifully built. Yet, when I survey the third type, foreign boats produced for the U.S. market, I keep my guard up every minute, for, beginning just after World War II and continuing into the present, builders all around the world have sent us boats with some incredibly bad construction details. Not an occasional bad boat, but whole fleets of them destined to fall apart with depressing predictability.

Strangely, this built-in self-destruction seems to have been at its worst in all-wooden boats and in boats with wooden decks and trunks on fiberglass hulls, both of which types were still being exported to this country well into the 1970s. Had these boats been built in countries with no wooden boatbuilding background, one could expect defective products, but the vast majority came from Scandinavia, other European countries, and some Asian countries where the trade has been plied for centuries if not millenia. Yet boats were sent here with mitered joints, which man has long known are by nature unable to stay closed in the marine environment. Stems, keels, and ribs were laminated with glues that failed in a decade or so. Scarfed planks and hollow masts also came unglued. Plywood that could not survive saturation was used. Fin keels were built up with lifts of wood between hull and iron ballast, using a wood so soft and splintery that, due either to the bending from side to side or the rust growing on the keel bolts, the lifts split open vertically down the centerline. Black iron (ungalvanized mild steel) fastenings or hardware were slipped into some boats in places where American builders would consider even galvanized parts to be a less desirable substitute for bronze, stainless, or Monel. Whether at the specification of the U.S. designers, agents, or promoters, or out of their own desire to cut costs, the builders of imports have often completely disregarded the world's ancient body of wisdom concerning the use of boatbuilding materials. In their defense, I know of one case where every detail of the construction was spelled out in plans and specifications by an engineer hired by the designer-dealer in this country, and there must be other, similar cases.

Many surveyors have suffered embarrassment and, sometimes, serious trouble due to the unwise use of wood in these boats. A friend of mine, one of the best in the business, was such a one. Hired to survey a six-year-old, one-owner, yard-maintained Scandinavian-built wooden IOR racer-cruiser sloop with glued-seam mahogany planking on steam-bent oak ribs, he found her in excellent condition except for two or three scattered broken ribs and a single fine, open glue seam just above the waterline in each topside. Two years later, when the second owner put her up for sale, another surveyor found those seams opened about a quarter inch, and a majority of the ribs broken in way of them. Seeing this, the prospective buyer took the next plane back to the other coast, and the second owner promptly filed suit against my friend for not warning him of these problems, which the first owner "must have caused." I was called upon to consult in the matter.

It was obvious to me that those breaks in the ribs were very recent, probably caused by the second owner's extralong seasons afloat and skimpier paint jobs. Coupled with the fact that he had stored her in a damp, leaky shed and caulked those open glue seams apart, it added up to her swelling further than ever before. Because of the way the boat was built, she simply couldn't stand a good soaking. I felt that her open seams were due to shrinking and her broken ribs due to swelling, and I was sure of it later when I spotted a sister ship in another yard with an almost identical set of open seams and broken ribs. These duplicate defects made it rather difficult to deny that, in truth, the potential for them was built into that line of boats. A standard plank-on-frame boat leaves room in its caulked seams for the planks to swell, but the construction used in this boat did not. Neither, apparently, were the planks edge-fastened. It is not the surveyor's province to advise of every possible manner in which a construction shortcoming might be aggravated by hard use or inappropriate maintenance procedures; his responsibility is to report on those flaws that have surfaced at the time of the survey. Anyway, this construction could apparently get by for a few years, especially with a short season, dry storage, and copious repainting, such as first owners would be likely to provide, but exposing that tightly fitted, glued mahogany planking to one or two cycles of going from tinder dry to saturation and back would burst the boat apart like ripe tomatoes after heavy rain. In the end, these facts helped my surveyor friend only to the extent that the second owner settled out of court for a modest sum.

In 1983 I was called upon to suggest repairs for the laminated plywood main deck of an IOR racer-cruiser built in Europe for its New England designer-dealer. The plywood was delaminating where its too-thin fiberglass covering had split and let water in. What made this a particularly tricky situation was the absence of anything else, such as deck beams, to maintain the boat's shape and integrity if the delaminated plywood were to be removed. Because it was supporting the cabin trunk, coamings, cockpit, hatches, deck hardware, and toerails, and was fastened to the hull at the sheer, replacement of this few hundred dollars' worth of plywood threatened to cost many thousands of dollars—a pretty disheartening turn of events when a boat is supposed to be of high-grade construction and is but 14 years old. I don't know what that plywood had in it for glue, but it sure wasn't up to our standards for "waterproof," "marine," or even "exterior."

The least expensive repair I could recommend was a new

fiberglass covering heavy enough to act as a fiberglass deck, well fastened to the failing plywood. I recommended that it be turned up against, rabbeted into, and well fastened to the cabin trunk sides and coamings.

In mid-1984, accompanied by a prospective buyer who is both an experienced boat owner and a professional engineer, I surveyed another boat of this same model and age. I knew from my first encounter with the model that if the thin fiberglass covering on the main deck hadn't been replaced, it was likely to be leaking water into the plywood. Sure enough, we found a number of spots where the fiberglass was fractured and the underlying plywood locally saturated. So far, there had been no appreciable delamination or rot in these areas, but there were two other signs that all was not well with this deck. A bedding strip or "corner molding" had been fitted against the base of the cabin trunk, and neither it nor the wood of the trunk adjacent to it would retain varnish. The base of the toerail was also rejecting varnish and was blackened by saturation. Obviously, while careful patching might keep this deck out of trouble for some more years, a new, more substantial covering would be the only sure way to head off serious deterioration.

The buyer and his wife were enthusiastic about the boat's design, size, and handsome joinerwork, and at first it looked as though they might push ahead with negotiations and the purchase despite the prospect of getting involved in a repair as extensive as recovering the deck. Unfortunately, the thin gelcoat was splitting apart in fine cracks all over the topsides, which would have to be sanded down to the underlying laminate and refinished. If the job were done in a yard using a sprayed finish of Awlgrip or Imron, the cost would range from $5,000 to $10,000. And there was more. A wedge-shaped welded-steel stand was positioned to support the bronze rudderport, a flax-packed stuffing box–bearing in the top of the port being bolted to the stand. By lying in the bottom of the cockpit seat locker and squinting into the narrow space between the cockpit sole and the hull abaft the fuel tank, I could see that the steel stand was a mass of rust. Besides being wasted itself, it was bursting open the glass attachment of its base to the hull. This mess was attributable to water dribbling from the stuffing box–bearing, which, like so many that are squeezed into an inaccessible corner with a steering quadrant close overhead, was in need of tightening or repacking and probably had been for the majority of its life. While checking the turning sheaves and the tension of the steering wires, I was astonished to notice that the cast-iron quadrant was also rusted, so thin in fact that the wire was coming through the bottoms of its grooves in places! Unheard of in a 15-year-old U.S.-built boat. Since the water hastening the disintegration of the quadrant could hardly have been spurting up onto it from the stuffing box below, there must have been a second source, either leaking through the deck plate for the emergency tiller or entering under the steering pedestal base.

The area was a ruin, and the job of reworking the iron stand so that it could be trusted to support the rudderport and bearing would be expensive because of its awkward location. "What a place to install ungalvanized cast iron and welded steel!" I grumbled.

"A great place," quipped the buyer, "because nobody sees them there."

I was glad he hadn't lost his sense of humor over the growing list of problems turning up in this craft. One other is worthy of mention here: There were rust streaks running down from cracks in the fiberglass around the ballast keel, adjacent to the centerboard pivot bolt hole. Not a terribly big defect, but one tricky to repair properly because the hole is actually two holes in the fiberglass-encased iron, one either side of the centerboard slot, meaning that one end of each hole penetrates the fiberglass up inside the slot. Not every boatyard's work on this type of problem remains watertight longer than a season or two, yet until it is made tight, rust will continue to grow and the cracks in the fiberglass shell will propagate, making this a perennial problem.

The cost at boatyard prices of putting this import back in shape would have been at least half the agreed price subject to survey. This buyer was not interested in either trying to renegotiate the price or enduring the hassle of getting the work done.

One Asian builder offers as an option "laid teak decks" over the decks of fiberglass boats. These are wearing out in less than a decade and wrecking the underlying plywood-cored fiberglass deck in the process. Opting for a teak deck from this company, it has turned out, is literally "buying trouble." Briefly stated, the trouble includes paper-thin wood plugs popping out and exposing the fastening heads, water working down through the fiberglass deck into the core of its sandwich laminate, and the (here we go again) nonwaterproof plywood core becoming saturated and delaminated.

Once the plywood core is spongy and the thin inner skin of the deck is leaking into the accommodations, there seem to be but two courses of repair to follow, after, of course, removing the guilty teak overlay: (1) Chop out and replace the core and inner skin of the fiberglass deck. This can be done either in place or after removing the entire molding from the hull, but either way it is very expensive. (2) Add enough new layers of fiberglass atop the existing outer deck laminate to restore watertight integrity and stiffness, but leave the inner skin and core alone. They will serve no further functional purpose, but once dry they will cause no problem, either. Regardless of which course is taken in the repair, the other choice to be made is between a new teak overlay and some other finish. Hopefully, if it is a new teak deck, history will not repeat itself.

As the reader has probably gathered, the builders of imports don't always use other boatbuilding materials any more judiciously than they do wood. I have encountered fiberglass that never cured; joinerwork with its fiberglass tabbing loose from the hull; strange concoctions of sand or other minerals mixed with too little resin and poured over and around the ballast in hollow keels, only to crumble in time and create a mess; integral tanks that leaked seawater or bilge water in, and fuel or fresh water out; rigs that let the mast go over the side on an otherwise pleasant summer afternoon sail; and hardware too small for the job or made of metal that was junk. The list is longer than that, but my point is that the percentage of imports with problems has been higher than that of U.S.-built boats, and the problems are, on the average, more serious, too.

I can't tell you whether imports have changed for better or for worse in recent years. A surveyor does not often get to see an import before it is 8 to 10 years old, when he makes a buyer's survey for the second owner or a condition survey for an insurance company. (While they take on new boats with little fuss, insurers usually require a survey to reassess condition in some year short of a decade.) Meanwhile, any defects in a boat seem to manifest themselves most unequivocally during a boat's teens nowadays. If those defects are only gelcoat problems, loose deck hardware and associated deck leaks, or wear in the rigging, steering, propulsion, or other systems, they can perhaps be forgiven, but it is a shocking condemnation of a boat's quality when parts of the structure are already disintegrating in what should be the early years of the boat's troublefree period, not the beginning of its *declining* years.

By the time a surveyor knows the true nature of a given model, it may no longer be in production. Or the builder may be out of business, or the company may have changed hands, nullifying any chance of even partial restitution. Prospective buyers should bear this in mind, along with the fact that foreign builders tend to be judgmentproof in civil action; their agents or dealers should be checked out to ascertain their financial stability and probable longevity, since the agent or dealer may be the only possible source of redress if the boat is a lemon.

One of the biggest yacht and commercial boatbuilders in the Orient, and one of the wiliest anywhere, never ships a yacht until it has received full payment in cash, flatly denies that defects are its fault, and doesn't worry at all about lawsuits because it is careful never to own anything in the United States that could be attached. In putting together his case, one owner hired me to study his fiberglass boat built by that company and to make recommendations for repair to a crucial area suffering from undercured resin. A year or two later, I met one of the principals of the conservative and honorable U.S. firm that had sold him the boat. "We got out of the boat dealer business," he said. "You know, that boat you wrote a report on cost us a small fortune."

Embarrassed for all of us, but mainly disgusted with the builder, I could only say, "I'm very sorry to hear that," for there is certainly no joy in seeing anyone lose money.

As I said, the surveyor's knowledge of imports tends to be more historical than current, but if history has a lesson, it is to be very wary of imported boats. For specific information about particular models, talk to as many knowledgeable people as possible and refer to the back issues of nonadvertising periodicals, in particular *The Telltale Compass* (12706 Kembridge Drive, Bowie, MD 20715) and *The Practical Sailor* (editorial offices: Box 819, Newport, RI 02840). The former newsletter was a monthly that ceased publication in 1985, and the latter is published twice monthly.

8

Sap from Fiberglass?

Mr. Joseph Brown's call was unusual in that he was the one out of perhaps 20 prospective boat buyers who asks questions about a surveyor's experience. He wanted to be sure that I was knowledgeable about fiberglass construction. After I allowed that I had built scores of fiberglass boats in my custom boatshop and had surveyed a good number of them, too, he said, "Well, here's my problem: I found a 36-foot, 13-year-old sloop that's just what my family and I want. We wouldn't be able to afford her except that the price is about $8,000 less than the Buc Book on this model and year. What worries me is that she is offered at that price 'as is, firm'—in other words, 'take it or leave it'—and I can't be sure whether the owner simply doesn't want to be bothered with negotiations or if there's something radically wrong with her. I would like to have you look her over very carefully, and I would like to be there when you do."

I agreed that the conditions of the sale made a survey seem especially desirable, assured Joe that his presence was welcome, and worked out a mutually agreeable date.

Twenty-four hours of rain had just ended when we met at the boat. Rain is always useful to help a surveyor discover deck leaks.

However, it had also brought huge puddles of water under this particular boat, still hauled out in winter storage, making it a gymnastic feat for me, suspended from the cradle's cross logs, to get a glimpse of the centerboard housed in the shallow ballast keel. It would be necessary to recommend that the board be inspected when the boat could be hoisted by the boatyard's lift. Meanwhile, the word we got from the men who worked in the yard, who had been maintaining the boat for some years, and whom I have known well for half a working lifetime, was that all was well with the board and its case as far as they knew, except that the wire pendant was due to be replaced.

As we went through the rest of the survey, the boat's construction turned out to be of good quality, normal in most details, and it had survived its 13 years very well both cosmetically and structurally except in one area. In way of the main cabin, the trunk and side decks had numerous leaks; there were also some stress cracks in the plasterlike finish of the overhead surfaces and an unusual flexibility in the trunk top when it was walked on. We did not discover all of these flaws at once. Joe had noticed the limberness of the trunk top on his first trip to the boat, and pointed it out when I was studying the deck. The deck leaks were evident as soon as we went below, thanks to still-damp runs or stains and an occasional drop of water from the recent rain. In the course of listing which hardware items the leaks were associated with (most of the leaks were through fastening holes), we noticed stress cracks along the interior corner of the trunk sides at deck level and in the underside of the trunk top around the hatches. The limberness of the trunk and these fine stress cracks were certainly related, but the leaks were due to the bedding under the hardware having lost its "life" over the years, or to loosened fastenings, or both. We noted that some pieces of hardware had recently been rebedded. These were not leaking.

While studying those details, we literally put our fingers on yet another problem. Here and there in the main cabin, a reddish-brown sticky substance was oozing from the interior surface of the trunk top and sides, the underside of the side decks, and the after bulkhead. This material was not dissimilar in nature to uncured resin or pine pitch. It appeared in droplets on the plasterlike finish of the laminate, and one was tempted to joke that perhaps God did make fiberglass trees, from whose wood this sap was oozing. In over 20 years of working with fiberglass I had not seen the material act like that! Certainly not when it was 13 years old. Perhaps, I ventured, here was the answer to the enigmatic price and sale conditions; perhaps the slightly too-flexible cabin trunk leaking around its hardware fastenings, showing stress cracks here and there, and exuding this sticky substance had spooked the owner into putting the boat on the market at a substantial discount, but with no guarantee. It was a situation demanding careful study and reflection on my part before I could express an opinion or make recommendations. It was one of those times when, alone, with naught to lean on but his own memory bank and logic, a surveyor must wring the best possible conclusions from the evidence, make his stand, and sweat the results.

We took a piece of hardware off the trunk top so that we could view the cross section of the laminate in its fastening holes. The layup consisted of about $3/16$ inch of gelcoat and fiberglass layers, with the plaster or finish coat on the interior bringing the total thickness to about $3/8$ inch. This interior coat was similar to microballoons or pecan shells in resin, off-white in color, fine in texture, and fairly hard, although neither flinty hard nor glossy like gelcoat. It was one solution to the perennial problem of finishing fiberglass interior surfaces; in place of wood, vinyl, fabric, or such, or a fiberglass liner, simply plaster it with a filled-resin product. An unusual solution, although hardly unique, it was very neatly done on this boat, giving precisely the effect of the fine plaster coat a shoreside plasterer might apply. "It wouldn't surprise me if professional plasterers were hired to do this," I mused, half to myself, remembering a couple of times when I had tried that at my own shop. "They have the knack of smoothing similar substances, although they did much better on a cement boat we built than they did on one we had covered with fiberglass."

It was this plastered area, exclusively, which we found to be exuding the sticky stuff. I considered it fortunate that the problem was limited to this area, for had the entire boat been bleeding, it would have been very difficult to stifle the fear that the structure was disintegrating. Needless to say, confined though it was to the main cabin, this set of problems became the focal point of the survey. The rest of the boat being quite acceptable, my responsibility devolved to assessing the gravity of this situation and developing a set of contingency plans for dealing with it, so that Joe could make a decision about consummating the purchase of the boat. My recommendations in the survey report follow. I have omitted the descriptive sections of the report.

COMMENTS: This boat is clean and neatly maintained, and has survived its 13 years very well except for deck leaks and whatever problems there may be with the centerboard, if any, both of which will be discussed in Recommendations. I would consider her a worthwhile investment at the agreed price, which I understand is fairly heavily discounted from the book value, and an investment that should increase markedly in value when her few problems are sorted out.

FAIR MARKET VALUE: 30,000 to 35,000 dollars.

REPLACEMENT VALUE: See current prices of equivalent boats.

INSURABLE VALUE: Same as fair market value.

RECOMMENDATIONS:

1) When the boat is on the Travelift, the centerboard should be lowered and thoroughly checked for soundness of the pivot pin, clearance between the board and case, and attachment and soundness of the pendant. It was noted that the centerboard winch is pulling away from the bridge deck and should be bolted more securely. The board should be well coated with appropriate preservative where steel, and the board and case should get antifouling treatment, too.

2) The most worrisome facet of this boat, which is quite normal in its construction in other details, is the combination of many deck leaks that have not been stemmed completely (although some hardware has recently been rebedded) and a limberness of the trunk top in the center of its unsupported area. To further complicate the situation, there are cracks in the overhead along the corner of the trunk sides to side deck and the juncture of hatch trim to the laminate; also, there are some drops of sticky substance oozing here and there from the interior of the trunk and deck laminate. Almost two out of the more

than four hours spent surveying this boat were concerned in some way with this unusual situation. The following are my most carefully drawn conclusions about the deck and trunk:

A. Judging from the places where we could inspect an edge of it, the deck laminate is substantial. When constructed, the deck and trunk, which are a one-piece part, were coated on the interior with a coat of resin containing a filler not unlike microballoons or pecan shell flour. This coating brought the total thickness of the laminate from perhaps ⅛ to ³/₁₆ inch of fiberglass to about ⁵/₁₆ to ⅜ inch in the trunk top, and no doubt more than that in the side decks. The coating was smoothed so that it was, when painted, a nicely finished interior overhead surface. The handrails and deck hardware were all bolted through this laminate. This deck molding is, then, a single-skin molding, reinforced and finished smooth with a plaster or putty of significant thickness.

B. In the life of the boat, three things have happened to this deck/ trunk part: The hardware has begun to leak, as have the hatch coamings and the skylight and the handrails, all of which is hardly surprising after 13 years of weathering. The trunk top in the middle of its unsupported span has become more flexible, probably, than when new, although all we know for sure is that it is a little more flexible than we are comfortable with now. If it has become more flexible over time, it may be due either to fine cracks that we cannot see (because of the paint on the overhead) in the putty/plaster, or to saturation of it by the deck leaks. Then there is the scattered oozing of sticky drops from the surface on the interior. This would seem to be some uncured resin product that is being displaced, again, by moisture penetrating or migrating through the putty/plaster and the paint.

C. In my opinion, the deck leaks can all be solved by rebedding the hardware, handrails, and hatch coamings. There is a good fiberglass laminate facing the weather which will not let moisture through anywhere but at holes through it.

The limberness of the trunk top, if it worsens, can be eliminated in either of two ways: by building in several deck beams or by fiberglassing the entire overhead with alternate mat and continuous-strand roving, the latter running athwartships. The deck beams are less costly than the fiberglass laminating, but neither is very expensive relative to the value of this boat.

The oozing or leaching of resin, I believe, will stop when the leaks are stopped and the overhead dried out, which may take some forced hot air or other heat treatment. Should it not stop, an application of well-catalyzed resin to the overhead (after removing the present paintlike coat, unless it is resin based) or of gelcoat should kick it over (cure it) and/or seal it off.

3) When the deck hardware is rebedded, backing plates should be added where there are none; larger plates can be substituted where plates now exist. Even large washers are a help to spread the pressure of the bolts over a greater area. Lifeline stanchion bases, winches, sheet blocks, and the mooring cleat are the items most in need of backing plates.

Naturally, everything that would be in the report and more had been discussed by the time the survey was completed. Agreeing with me that repairs to whatever might be wrong with this boat could hardly cost more than the generous discount in her price, Joe made up his mind to buy her. I would have done the same in his place, yet it is much easier to make such a decision for one's own account than to advise someone else to do it.

Little did I know that in two months I would be surveying another sloop by the same designer and the same builder, somewhat smaller and one year older than Joe's boat, with her main cabin finished in the same way, and, not too surprisingly, also oozing "sap."

The asking price was par for that model, according to the Buc Book, but Donald Smith had been able to negotiate an agreed price that was discounted just about as much as Joe's had been. The close relationship of the two boats became evident when, as Don drove us to the survey in Connecticut, I read the broker's listing to familiarize myself with his prospective purchase. Of course, I did not yet know whether this boat had the same interior finish, or whether the "sap" was running.

Don liked the boat. Her shoal draft, due to a centerboard through an external ballast keel, was appropriate for the waters of Nasketucket Bay, Massachusetts, where he would moor her, and she would be a real joy when looking for a place to anchor in many of the shallow crowded harbors that weekenders like to frequent across Buzzards Bay on the shores of Cape Cod and the Elizabeth Islands. I had to concur that the boat's specifications seemed ideal for his yachting requirements, and that the agreed price was excellent if the survey went well.

When we arrived at the boatyard, the owner had opened up the boat and had arranged with the yard to lift her later in the morning for inspection of the centerboard and its case, so that I was able to plunge right into the survey. Studying this boat, designed by the designer of Joe's boat and built one year earlier by the same builder, brought out similarities and differences in their construction that I, as a boatbuilder, found intriguing. What inspiration, notion, success, failure, shortage, or cost consideration caused a given detail to be retained or altered from the boats of one year to those of the next? Although very similar in model to Joe's boat, this boat had a welded, hollow, aluminum rudder on a stainless steel stock, while Joe's had a fiberglass rudder on a bronze stock. I asked whether two threaded holes in the blade were for machine screws that had held on a sacrificial zinc. This the owner verified, saying that he was in the habit of obtaining a new zinc for the spot every year. From the edges of these holes it could be seen that the blade was constructed of ⅛-inch plate.

Both boats had the same type of exhaust system, a water-jacketed section from the engine to a high, dry loop, with the water injected into the after leg. From there, steam hose and a rubber muffler carried the water and gasses to the stern. The water-jacketed section in Joe's boat was copper, whereas in this earlier boat it was stainless. Was the switch to copper due to the habit stainless has of cracking when subjected to vibration? I wouldn't have been a bit surprised, for some did on boats I built when they were attached directly to the engine, without a flexible section to isolate them. At the same time, here was the system on Don's prospective purchase still working after 14 years.

Perhaps the most noticeable difference between the two boats was the lavish use of aluminum on this boat, including the tiller hardware, stemhead fitting, chainplates, genoa tracks or rails, lifeline stanchion bases, mast step, cleats, and, as mentioned, the rudder blade. That many of these items were bronze or stainless steel on Joe's boat a year later seemed to indicate that there had been a retreat from a too-exuberant use of aluminum to a more commonsense approach. No question, the most daring or dangerous use of the metal had been in the chainplates and the stemhead fitting, for there it was subjected to both heavy strains and severe corrosive conditions. Examination of the holes for the turnbuckle pins showed ovalization at the top as well as chamfering of the edges, from corrosion. After one look at this I announced that I was sure the turnbuckles must be bronze and responsible for the corrosion. When we went to look at the standing rigging on the mast, on horses by the spar shed, I was chagrined to see that the turnbuckles were silver colored; before I could make any apologies, however, it became apparent that they were indeed bronze, but chrome plated. At the same time, they did have stainless steel clevis pins. In summary, corrosion had attacked the chainplates, but attrition was only at the rate of about ¼ inch at the bearing point in 14 years, probably because of the stainless pins and the chrome plating on the bronze turnbuckles, now worn off in places.

It would be necessary in my report to mention the many aluminum items on this boat with a general warning that they should be guarded from corrosion, and perhaps make some particular suggestions for maintaining the rudder and the chainplates. That aspect of this particular survey was made easier for me by the fact that Don's business involved metal fabrication, for I knew that he could handle any needed metalwork.

Interestingly, when I later told the broker about the chainplates and turnbuckles, he said, "It's hard to believe that the boat was designed and built that way. Are you sure those chainplates are not stainless steel? We have a boat of that same model right here in the yard. Let's have a look."

To his surprise, the boat, about a hundred feet from his office, had aluminum chainplates. More surprising to all of us, the clevis pin eyes were ovalized upward at least ¼ inch, and when we trooped out to the spar shed we found a set of chrome-plated bronze turnbuckles on her standing rigging.

Among the recommendations I ultimately submitted with my report, the aluminum hardware, while not posing a terribly serious problem, was nevertheless foremost except for the "sap" oozing out of her main cabin's interior plaster. One had to assume that the oozing was to some extent responsible for the sizable discount from the asking price that Don had been able to negotiate. Was this oozing business a symptom of a more destructive condition than it seemed? On the way home, I outlined my opinion of the condition, much as stated in item 4 of the Recommendations. I still believed that porosity in the plaster, allowing moisture to penetrate, was the cause, much as water penetrating porous gelcoat has been found to be the cause of "boat pox." Since the plaster was of a texture that should dry out and accept paint with a minimum of sanding off its surface (unlike the gelcoat, which traps moisture within and therefore has to be removed), it ought not to be a big project, I reasoned, to thoroughly dry out these surfaces and then seal them against further penetration by moisture.

I pointed out to Don as I had to Joe that the saving in the price of this boat, compared with the price of similar boats, gave him a spread of several thousand dollars with which to work. The very worst that could happen, in my opinion, would be the necessity of applying paint, more laminate, or both to the cabin trunk area. That seemed reasonable to him, and having been inclined to do so anyway because of all its other desirable aspects, he bought the boat.

Following are the recommendations I included in my survey report.

RECOMMENDATIONS:

1) There is considerable aluminum hardware on this boat, including the rudder blade, the rudder stuffing box, the stemhead fitting, chainplates, genoa "tracks" or rails, lifeline stanchion bases, spars, mast step, and numerous cleats. I would think these to have been made of mostly high-grade aluminum; otherwise, they would have needed more replacements than there seem to have been. However, it would be wise to keep an eye out for signs of corrosion at all times, to keep other metals except stainless steel out of contact with the aluminum, and to protect the aluminum parts with epoxy or other coatings wherever practicable.

In the case of the rudder, I would look into an epoxy coating as a primer under the antifouling, or an epoxy-based antifouling paint, or one of the coatings used on the aluminum lower units of outboards and outdrives.

2) The chainplates are beginning to show corrosion around the clevis holes, despite the fact that the pins themselves are stainless. I reason that the bronze turnbuckles above the plates are causing this. Originally these were plated, and perhaps this inhibited the action in

the boat's early years. Replacement with all stainless parts would minimize future corrosion.

Meanwhile, coating the turnbuckles with heavy waterproof grease and taping on a plastic bag or wrapping to keep the salt water off them after they are shaken down would do the same thing, much as we used to wrap galvanized turnbuckles to keep them from rusting.

If in the future these chainplates should become a worry, it would not be difficult or expensive to cut them off and grind them back just below the deck surface, and install new stainless plates right alongside the old ones on the outside of the fiberglass with which they're wrapped, after flattening out the lumpiness. If this were done, I would put the forward-tending lower and aft-tending lower on the forward and after sides of their old chainplates, respectively, to increase, not diminish the spread. The upper shrouds' new chainplates might have to be joggled or offset to keep them in line with the center of the mast. If not kept in line, uppers can cause the spreaders to buckle and collapse.

3) Some of the wiring is fastened to the bulkhead with iron staples, and some is loosely run. It would be good to tie or clip it neatly using nylon ties and clips.

The backside of the electrical panel is rather exposed both to dampness and physical damage in that port cockpit locker. A quickly removable cover would be a wise investment.

In the same area, it would be safer to install some hooks or chocks for any heavy objects such as spare anchors that will be kept there so that the exhaust system and other fittings and hoses don't get clobbered by shifting weights.

4) The "sap" oozing from the overhead is something noted before on a boat from this designer and builder. The filled resin plaster with which they smoothed and stiffened their overheads seems to react with water and give off this sticky stuff. The other boat was much worse; it had many deck leaks which were obviously feeding dampness into the plaster, and the boat was not covered in the winter, which I think is a great mistake. I don't know whether this boat has been covered, but I suspect it has not been kept dry, and I think probably the ooze will stop if (1) the boat is covered for the winter; (2) the nonskid areas of the deck and trunktop gelcoat are epoxy painted (perhaps not necessary if no porosity can be detected); (3) the interior is dried out, washed off with acetone, and coated with a well-catalyzed polyester resin–based material.

5) The propeller is smaller both in diameter and pitch by one inch for a boat of this size to be driven by an Atomic Four. I have seen many boats up to 10 or 12 thousand pounds that were able to swing a 13" x 8". Anyway, the thing to do is to see how the boat goes with this wheel, and whether the engine runs up too easily to its higher speeds. There is no need of overloading the engine, but you might be able to get more out of it if the boat is not already towing a wave.

6) There is a small break in the port toerail that ought to be fixed before something catches on it and makes it worse. The teak on deck could use some protection.

7) It would be good, for the intended cruising area, to obtain a spare anchor with a little more weight and holding power than that 13 lb. Danforth.

8) Being in the metalworking business, it should be easy for you to make up some backing plates of substantial stainless steel, and I would suggest a program of installing these wherever stanchion bases, cleats, or other hardware seem to need more backup.

9) As you know, welding aluminum tends to reduce it to zero temper. I don't know what that means in terms of the strength or stiffness of the metal in the mast, but I'd watch the welded spreader area for a while to see if it shows any sign of bending under sail. It ought to be all right, but you could soon tell if it were "giving" at all, I would think.

9

Part by Part: What to Look for in a Fiberglass Boat

In this chapter we will run through a list of what to look for in a fiberglass boat you are assessing. The order in which the parts are listed is a compromise between one that makes sense to a reader and the one in which I almost always view the parts of a boat during a survey, scrutinizing it first from the ground, next the deck, and then the interior, and finally examining the hardware, gear, and rig.

HULL AND DECK

Everyone, it seems, expects that a fiberglass hull, except where covered with bottom paint, should be a flawless expanse of shiny smoothness and unblemished color. Because of this attitude, the surveyor must inspect topsides closely even when they are in near perfect condition. A general statement about their cosmetic condition relative to the age of the boat is not enough; he should also mention specific scratches and dings, noting their locations, severity, and recommended treatment. The more perfect the surface as a whole, the more deserving of mention each flaw becomes, for the more likely a fastidious buyer is to complain about any oversight. "You know, there's another scratch that you didn't mention, aft on the starboard side."

Strange as it may seem to those of us who are mechanically oriented, some people are much more upset by a scratch in the topsides than by water dripping out of the keel. A boat is universally admired and prized for being good to look at, but some people are perfectionists.

It helps if the surveyor can state whether a given scratch, or a set of them, can merely be polished out, or must be filled with gelcoat putty and then polished, or, due to fractures in the underlying glass fibers, will require either a strong putty such as Marine-Tex or grinding out and rebuilding with a patch of fiberglass laminate. It gives the prospective buyer a clue to the probable cost of correcting the condition.

Treatment of problems within the gelcoat itself—crazing, alligatoring, star cracks, or stress cracks—can be difficult to recommend to a buyer even when the surveyor is sure in his own mind how the problems developed and what can be expected of them in the future. There are often many options for treating them, some worth a try but not certain to last, others surefire but expensive. The trick is to explain the situation clearly and then let a buyer make his own choice. When the gelcoat is beyond rejuvenation, it is nice to know, nowadays, that repainting the topsides (rather than regelcoating them, as was thought almost mandatory a decade ago) has become a comparatively inexpensive and widely accepted treatment. Some of the new paints rival gelcoat in appearance and last a number of years. True, none that I know of last more than about half as long as gelcoat, but they still work out to be less expensive in the long run.

Speculation though it may be, a surveyor does well to explain the likely cause or causes of gelcoat problems. This helps to keep the buyer from imagining something worse than the truth, possibly turning down the boat in a panic or being sold an overly drastic treatment by unscrupulous repairers.

In essence, an alligatored or "dried mud" pattern in gelcoat is due to shrinkage of the gelcoat itself, often because it was applied too thickly. Fine, sharp-edged cracks in the gelcoat radiating from a central dent or spot, called star cracks, are due to a concentrated

Here and opposite: *A selection of fiberglass hull-deck joints. (The common type in which the deck fits into a turned-in, rabbeted hull flange is pictured in Chapter 3.) The best joints are simply those that are well fastened, have live (still flexible) bedding, are fiberglassed over either inside or out, and are not leaking or (heaven forbid) separating.*

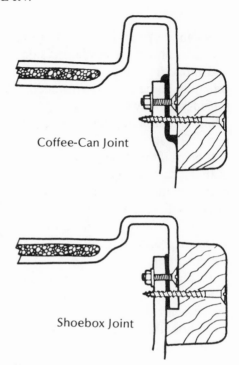

Coffee-Can Joint

Shoebox Joint

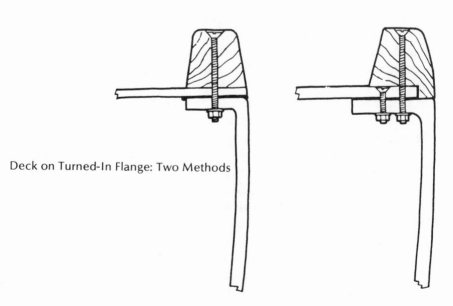

Deck on Turned-In Flange: Two Methods

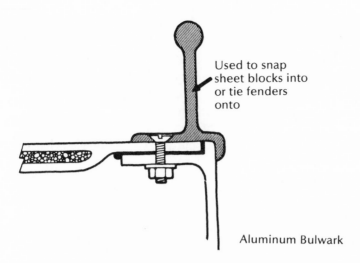

Used to snap sheet blocks into or tie fenders onto

Aluminum Bulwark

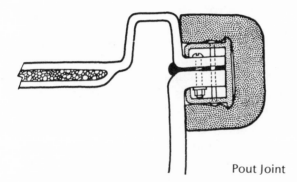

Pout Joint

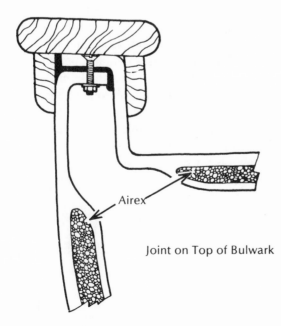

Airex

Joint on Top of Bulwark

stress or blow on the part. The stress could be from too much of the boat's weight bearing on the small area of a single support, and a blow could be from almost anything. The same sort of pattern with dulled edges and no real cracks is but the imprint of a star crack in the mold. (Molds are sometimes beaten mercilessly with rubber hammers, like some stubborn beast of burden, to get them to release the part.)

Fine, more or less parallel cracks are due to overbending of the underlying laminate, and they tend to run normal or perpendicular to the direction of the bend (parallel to its axis). They are found wherever heavy weights or pressures deform the part, which can happen anywhere on the flexible laminates of ultralight craft. When the laminates are thicker and stiffer, any stress cracks are more likely to be found along the corners where the laminate changes direction; that is to say, they show up along or parallel to the stiffened edges of a panel. Stress cracks are very rare on a well-built hull, only appearing where the boat has been subjected to excessive pressure that has locally tortured the laminate. Typical examples of this include stress cracks in the topsides of a boat that has been squeezed against a pier by heavier boats tied up outboard of her, and cracks on either or both sides along the juncture of hull and keel—a fin keel especially—when that member has had a severe lateral wrench or shock.

It can be difficult to determine whether or not the laminate beneath stress-cracked gelcoat has been damaged. It is often as good as the day it was laid up, having been bent more than the gelcoat could stand but not to its own yield point, and it might be able to endure indefinitely, without suffering damage, bending of the sort that cracked the gelcoat. On the other hand, the laminate might have fine cracks running through it, appreciably weakening it, and it may not be watertight. The tests for a weakened laminate:

1) The spot may be noticeably more flexible than the surrounding area when pressure is applied to it.

2) Tapping with a hard object or light hammer may disclose a difference in resonance between the fractured spot and adjacent areas.

3) If the back or inboard surface of the laminate is accessible for examination, it may show some whitish fracture lines; in extreme cases, the laminate may actually be delaminated inward.

Snow and ice like this will take any deck apart in time. My survey recommendations often include warnings to owners or prospective buyers about improper winter storage. Lack of an adequate boat cover is one of the biggest oversights. Others include an improper load-bearing distribution in the cradle and improper trim, which may cause rain or condensation to gather on deck rather than draining overboard.

If any sign of weakness is detected in the laminate, it should be reinforced with additional layers, or by grinding out and rebuilding the damaged portion, or both. Even if there is no sign of damage, reinforcing the laminate locally may be desirable. Otherwise the gelcoat, once repaired, will crack again when the forces that caused the original damage are again applied to the laminate. Only if the force that caused the gelcoat cracks was a onetime thing not likely to be repeated is a gelcoat repair likely to last. If the stress is bound to recur, the underlying laminate will have to be stiffened with additional layers or perhaps with a stiffener of glassed-over core material.

Stress cracks and star cracks are much more common on decks than on hulls, for decks have relatively flat surfaces subjected to high local loads and impacts, not the least of which are imparted by crew leaping down from piers, stomping around, and dropping heavy objects. Some extremely heavy loads can be applied by lifeline stanchion bases, sheet blocks, winches, and cleats, and it is not unusual to find cracks in the gelcoat around any of these. Walloping a pier with the deck edge or bulwark can result in stress cracks along the deck's waterways. Other stress cracks, along the juncture of cabin trunk and deck, coamings and seats, or seats and cockpit sole, all mean that the structure is being wracked by one force or another. Perhaps the most frequently occurring set of stress cracks is at the juncture of a cabin trunk and a cockpit coaming that is lower in height. It is not hard to see why if you think of the trunk side and coaming as a continuous girder supporting the deck. This point where the height changes, with a commensurate change in stiffness, is where the girder will yield first to bending forces on the deck structure, and the first signs of yielding are stress cracks. Stress cracks may also show up on deck at the forward end of the cabin trunk or the after end of the coaming, because these points mark the end of the girder.

When stress cracks appear around deck hardware, a larger, stiffer backing plate under the laminate is often all that is needed to prevent the overbending that is cracking the gelcoat. Indeed, when there is a liner in the overhead, a bigger backing plate may be the only reinforcement that can be provided neatly without making a big project of it. In some cases, especially when a sandwich construction is involved, a larger pad or base on deck as well as belowdeck will help to disperse the strains on the laminate.

Given a laminate that is just too light and is not likely to carry the required loads without recurring stress cracks or worse, it will be necessary to add reinforcing layers, more bracing, or both. Neither should a surveyor advise a prospective buyer to take on a boat that has been built so flimsily or driven so hard that she has stress cracks and incipient laminate fractures in many places, unless the buyer realizes that she will need ongoing reinforcement. The condition is not exactly rare. There are whole fleets of one-design racing boats like that, and plenty of lightly built racer-cruisers, too. After a few years of hard racing there's always some new break that needs patching on these boats, which are literally cracking up. I keep my guard up when surveying lightly built fiberglass boats.

By far the most common flaw in decks is the "breakout" of

This rudder's laminate is cracking up. Perhaps water got inside and froze, expanding enough to crack the shell, or perhaps the metal turning arms welded to the stock distorted the fiberglass (either because the laminate isn't heavy enough or the filler isn't solid enough).

bubbles under the gelcoat. These appear mainly on the top corners of coamings and toerails and on cockpit seat and hatch edges—wherever the underlying laminate does not continuously contact the backside of the gelcoat. The source of the problem can be traced to the molding of the part: Wet fiberglass is resilient and tends to "bridge" or spring up out of sharp recesses and corners, leaving an air space or bubble. Being brittle, the unsupported gelcoat over these spaces is very easily broken, exposing the laminate beneath. This is strictly a cosmetic problem, but a most unsightly interruption of the glossy surface. Further, the color of the surrounding gelcoat is not always easily matched. Potential breakouts can be revealed by tapping along likely locations with a coin or other hard, light object. Pound heavily and you will break them out, but one should resist the temptation if not invited to do so! There are, of course, more likely to be future breakouts on a new boat than an old one, for as the years go by the chances of a remaining, unbroken bubble grow slimmer.

Water dripping out of the hull anywhere should be carefully investigated, for where it is leaking out, it can leak in. Many production builders are too much in a hurry even to put a few pounds of filled resin in the lower, after corner of a hollow keel to prevent the bolts of the rudderheel fitting in a sailboat or a metal skeg in a powerboat from passing water into the interior. They would rather take a chance on bedding or sealant under the fitting or around the bolts, but you can see these fittings weeping on boat after boat in storage yards, and now and then you read about a boat that sank after "losing her steering" and being flooded from aft. It's fairly easy to open a sizable hole in a hollow fiberglass keel.

Any water coming in contact with strands of fiberglass that were not thoroughly saturated with resin during the layup will tend to "wick" or travel along those strands, sometimes producing leaks in remote and baffling locations. I was once mystified by a leak alongside the centerboard case of a boat; the water leaked in there when the boat was afloat but did not leak out at that spot when the boat was ashore. Just by chance, when the boat was moved, a small trickle was noticed coming out of the skeg at a point 10 feet from the inside leak and not directly beneath the bilge water. The water was covering that 10-foot distance through tiny tubes of unsaturated woven roving in the middle of the laminate along the hull-to-keel junction (what would be the garboard seam of a wooden boat).

A leak due to wicking is not common because only a small percentage of fiberglass boats contain resin-starved fibers, and even in those that do the unsaturated strands are likely to be sealed off from the exterior surface, the interior surface, or both, by intervening watertight layers and by gelcoat. In the above case, I believe the rudder gudgeon bolt holes in the skeg gave water access to the wick, but I never did learn the reason for it coming out where it did on the interior; my shop just sealed off both ends with fresh patches of well-saturated fiberglass. Wicking is one of those "it *has* happened" phenomena, sired by Murphy's Law, that should be tucked away in the surveyor's memory as a possible explanation of mysterious leaks. Other explanations include undercured resin, waterlogged cores (including leaks in the overhead from a waterlogged sandwich), and remote fractures caused by severe impacts.

I am very wary when I know that a hull has a balsa core, having seen some disastrous results of this construction in the past. I don't even like to see the stuff in decks. It is true that thousands upon thousands of boats have gotten along fine with balsa-cored decks for a number of years, but sooner or later every surveyor finds some number of them in trouble due to delamination, saturation with water, or both. Boats long thought to be doing fine are, at 15 to 20 years of age, developing spongy foredecks or sidedecks as water finally penetrates the outer skin and saturates the balsa core. I have seen this on several boats recently. Anyway, the percentage of balsa-cored hulls in which surveyors find problems is much greater than that of decks, and at least one American company has gone out of business partly because of trouble with their balsa-cored hulls.

Boats that are wholly or partly laid up in two pieces and then joined down the centerline need careful inspection of that joint. A few boats built this way have split open, and at least one drowning because of it made headlines across much of the country. When a stout job of joining has been done by a good builder, these boats seem as tough and durable as any, but now and then, from going aground or from the strains and shocks of being improperly supported, lifted, or, yes, dropped during hauling, one will open up. The repair itself is not difficult, but it is usually made expensive by restricted access to the area from the inside and by the need to fair in and refinish any patching layers applied on the outside. Should the split be in way of an integral fuel tank the job will be still more expensive, for then the fuel must be drained and the tank steam-cleaned or washed out with solvent to get a decent bond of the patching layers to the laminate. Meanwhile, access to the interior of the tank can only be through a hand hole, which itself may have to be cut out of the side of the keel or hull or the top of the tank.

While inspecting the bottom of a sailboat with a fin keel bolted to a canoe-bodied hull, the centerline area of the hull just forward of and abaft the keel should be examined for signs of athwartships cracks in the hull shell, the result of striking the bottom or a rock when underway. In several such accidents with which I am familiar,

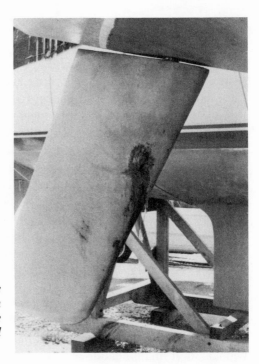

Iron rusting inside this rudder has erupted through its skin. It will get worse unless the rudder is sealed up absolutely tight again.

the relatively heavy centerline laminate was fractured all the way through and began leaking. On some boats this happened only at the after end of the keel, but others were damaged at both ends. Here again, dismantling joinerwork or cutting through soles and tanks to expose these areas on the inside, so that reinforcing layers can be built up over them, can make the repair expensive. In some cases the cost to repair a simple break, one that takes but a few hundred dollars to grind out and rebuild both inside and out, will escalate to a thousand or two by the time the interior is opened up locally and put back together afterward.

External ballast keels and their bolts have not given much trouble that I have seen. Most builders have learned to bury the inboard ends of the bolts, nuts, and washers under filled resin putty and fiberglass. On older models having a cast iron keel with the bolted flange left exposed, the heads of the bolts are likely to have rusted away, making it necessary to recommend replacing them. In later models with such keels, some builders are providing a recess in the hull into which the flange fits deeply enough to be covered and faired over with one fiberglass product or another. Only time will tell us how much longer the bolt heads will last, but if well encapsulated they should survive for many additional decades.

Ballast keels installed inside full, hollow fiberglass keels don't seem to get into too much trouble as long as they are well sealed over so that no bilge water can work down around them, freeze, and blow out the fiberglass casing. I was embarrassed recently when the buyer of a boat I had surveyed spruced her up handsomely and launched her only to have her leak copiously. When she was hauled out, the water ran out through a split in her fiberglass keel; there it had entered and had gone up through the layers that were supposed to seal off the ballasted portion from the bilge. He didn't blame me too much, because he found that the split was hidden from sight by a cross log of the cradle. I blamed myself, however, because I hadn't suspected a leak when I found this boat's bilge perfectly dry after she had spent a year on her cradle under a canvas cover so short it exposed both her foredeck and cockpit to driving rain. To a surveyor, anything unusual should be suspect—even a dry bilge when a boat would be expected to collect a little water.

A centerboard case and the boat itself can hardly be studied well enough from below without picking the boat up and lowering the board down. Fortunately, the lifts that most boatyards have today make this a quicker and relatively less expensive job than it used to be. Still, lifting her is an added expense, and if the boat is tucked away in storage where other boats block access to her, it may be out of the question at the time of the survey. For those reasons, it is not unusual to put off the final inspection of board and case until the boat is being readied for launching. The surveyor studies them as best he can at the survey, reservations about their condition are made in his report and in the sales agreement, and, possibly, an appropriate portion of the purchase price is put in escrow.

The three critical points for inspection around the board are its lower after corner, which strikes the bottom first; the attachment of the pendant, which constantly bears over half the weight of the board and must live underwater much of the time; and the pivot pin and its bearing in the board, another focal point of fairly constant weight, wear, and corrosion. The condition of pivot pin and bearing

The little things: The minute a surveyor sees this rudder, he is going to ask what keeps it from being unshipped if it is bumped on a rock. The owner admitted that it once came out and was towed, luckily, by the mizzen sheet until he could retrieve it. Normally, removable blocks fitted to the rudder below the gudgeon prevent upward movement. (Courtesy Elen Boat Works)

is difficult if not impossible to see without removing the board altogether, but an indication of the amount of wear is given by the amount the board can be jiggled about the pin. If it can be rattled up and down and fore and aft too much for ease of mind, it is time to pull the pin and see why.

The centerboard case should be inspected for signs of wear, damage to the laminate, or cracks, but I must say that, except in small, open racing boats that are lightly built and subject to hard campaigning, fiberglass cases have given much less trouble than wooden ones. In many boats where a ballast keel houses much of the board, the case is subject to minimal stress and wear, is located entirely below the top of the hollow fiberglass keel, and is so well sealed off from the interior that it can hardly present any leaking problem except through the tube that carries its pendant.

If cases that don't leak seem to take the adventure out of surveying centerboard boats, some of it has been returned by the deep, narrow boards that are raised and lowered with a pendant fitting in a groove over their rounded tops. In one boat I surveyed, the pendant had jumped out of the groove and had jammed the board in the down position; as a result (I was amazed to note when I crawled under the boat), the board was broken off flush with the bottom of the keel. There are also plenty of potential problems with the pendant itself, which, after rounding the board, exits the case through a stuffing box headed forward, makes a 180-degree turn to run aft under the length of the cabin sole, then turns roughly 90 degrees up to a winch in way of the cockpit. All of these features, dedicated to a "more efficient" deep and narrow board that intrudes not the slightest into the "living space," are items for the surveyor's attention both from outside and inside the boat.

When the hull's exterior is studied, all of the through hulls should be checked. On fiberglass boats I have found few if any with problems much worse than being almost plugged up with marine life or being a bit loosened and weeping where they pass through the hull. Except when attacked by powerful electrolysis, standard American-made bronze through hulls last a lot longer than fiberglass has been around. The Delrin ones don't have an electrolysis problem but are more easily cracked.

A fiberglass tube glassed to the hull, and usually connected to a hose, is used by more and more builders wherever seacocks or valves are not considered necessary and for shaft logs and rudder-ports. These through hulls are the least likely of any to leak at their hull junctions. Metal tubes fiberglassed to the hull, however, do not very often remain watertight along the interface of metal and fiberglass; one day the surveyor will find such a joint weeping or, if the boat is hauled out, will note a telltale stain running away from it. In a typical case, some builders of tiller-steered sailboats will fiberglass a metal tube to the hull and to the cockpit sole as a rudderport for the metal stock. I have found a number of these tubes to have worked loose at one end or both. The appropriate recommendation is simple enough: Cover the whole tube with fiberglass, as it should have been in the first place; then it can't get away, and it can't leak.

RUDDER

Metal rudders still predominate on powerboats, while most all builders of fiberglass sailboats have gone to fiberglass rudders. Nevertheless, a number of early fiberglass boats with wooden rudders are still around. Only yesterday I saw a worker covering with fiberglass the wooden rudder of a boat built in the 1950s. Incidentally, fiberglass rudders for custom boats are usually made in just that way, by wrapping a core with fiberglass, although materials other than wood, such as the rigid foams, are used more and more for the core.

Production builders generally mold their rudders in two pieces or "half shells" that are assembled around the metal rudder stock, if there is one, with a filler of reinforced casting resin. The filler, when it hardens, glues everything together. To save weight, some builders insert a core of very light material that displaces most of the resin-based filler, leaving only a narrow band of it around the edges of the rudder to glue and seal the centerline joint. This practice may leave voids inside the blade into which water eventually penetrates; in cold climates it will freeze, splitting the blade open along the joint. I've seen enough of these split rudders to want to inspect every production rudder very carefully.

When the rudder is hung outboard, one can wrap up the entire rudder story in one session. In question are:

1) The soundness of the rudder itself, and its adequacy for the size of the boat.

2) The strength, appropriateness, and amount of wear or wasting from corrosion of the metal hardware and its fastenings.

3) The attachment of the tiller—or tiller arm if there is a steerer—and the degree of play in the system or twist in the rudder itself when the helm is prevented from moving while pressure is put on the blade.

4) Whether the rudder is so hung as to resist being unshipped if it is lifted when taking the ground. If so, the rudder will be prone to damage should the boat ever strike bottom.

5) Whether there are adequate stops to prevent damage should the rudder be slammed hard over with great force, as can happen when one loses control of the helm while backing down.

The same concerns apply to an inboard rudder hung against a rudder post or skeg. In this case there is, in addition, the need to study the rudderport both as a bearing for the stock and as a means

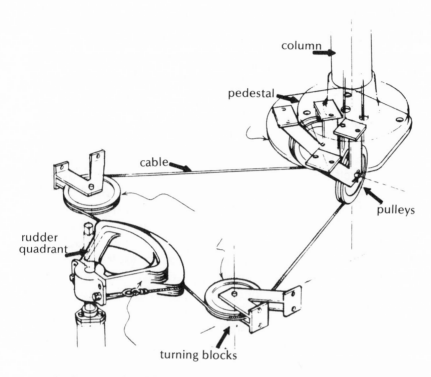

A chain and cable steering system with a pedestal steerer, a common configuration for aft-cockpit sailboats. The wheel shaft is fitted with a chain sprocket to drive the chain, the ends of which are connected inside the steering column to the cable ends. The cables exit below the pedestal as shown. Too much play in the cables, vertical misalignment of turning blocks and rudder quadrant, and loosening of the turning blocks are the most frequent problems. (Courtesy the Edson Corp., New Bedford, Massachusetts)

of excluding water from the boat, whether by height above the waterline, by a stuffing box, or both.

If the inboard rudder is a spade rudder, especially an all-metal one, its outside-the-boat parts will be fairly simple to inspect, but one's study on the interior must include concern about the strength of the rudderport and the upper bearing, if there is one. A surveyor should ask himself whether the rudder stock will bend if the blade is subject to enough force, or whether it is more likely to tear a hole in the boat. If holing the boat is more a probability than a possibility, the fact should be mentioned in the report along with a recommended remedy (which would probably be a local reinforcing of the hull).

STEERING SYSTEM

It's a pleasure to see a tiller fitted snugly to the head of an outboard rudder or to well-designed hardware on an inboard rudder's stock, so that the slightest movement of the helm is transmitted smoothly by the rudder into pressure against the water. On too many boats, a disconcerting rattle, often better described as a clunk-clunk, disrupts this simple action so central to the enjoyment of sailing. The ridiculous aspect of the condition is that the wear of wood or metal that has occurred, such as a badly ovalized pivot bolt hole, could usually have been avoided by such simple measures as dabbing with grease and tightening the bolt.

Similar play is likely in wheel steering systems, of which about 80 percent currently use a drive train based on wire rope. Most of the time the play in these systems is due to nothing more than slack wire, and the slack, in turn, is due to nothing more than stretch, and a means of adjusting wire tension is provided. Mushy steering aside, it is important to recommend that obvious, drooping slack be taken up before the wire jumps the groove in a sheave or the quadrant and fouls up the system.

Naturally, any part of these steering systems that the surveyor can reasonably get at should be studied for signs of the other problems they occasionally develop. The most common big problem is loosening of the turning blocks. It seems that builders are forever underestimating the strength required in these blocks and their attachment to the hull. Once in awhile one finds that a misalignment was set up in the system by the builder or a later repairer; cheek blocks were improperly positioned or the quadrant was set too high or too low on the rudder stock.

When there is no upper bearing for the rudder stock and too much unsupported height, one can often see the stock bending under the pressure of the steerer. This condition will bring serious trouble

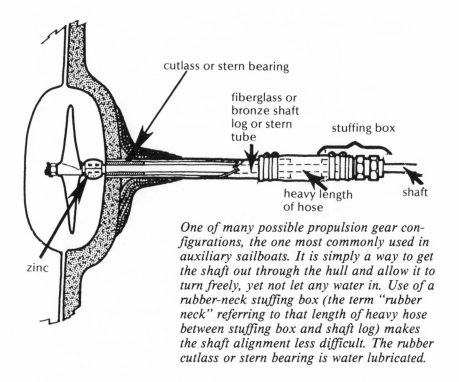

cutlass or stern bearing

fiberglass or
bronze shaft
log or stern
tube

stuffing box

heavy length
of hose

shaft

zinc

One of many possible propulsion gear con-
figurations, the one most commonly used in
auxiliary sailboats. It is simply a way to get
the shaft out through the hull and allow it to
turn freely, yet not let any water in. Use of a
rubber-neck stuffing box (the term "rubber
neck" referring to that length of heavy hose
between stuffing box and shaft log) makes
the shaft alignment less difficult. The rubber
cutlass or stern bearing is water lubricated.

sooner or later, and the surveyor should not hesitate to recommend
that an upper bearing be installed even though it may require an
extension of the stock with a muff coupling to the overhead, or some
construction to support the bearing.

Badly worn rudder bearings, no matter the type, will sometimes
cause a "clunk" every time the direction of the helm is changed,
making one think there is something wrong with the steerer. That's
why attacking the rudder to check for movement within its bearings,
even with a timber used as a pry, is very important on any boat.

The surveyor should not overlook the steering wheel, the shaft, its
bearings, and the sprocket and length of chain (or, sometimes, the
wire drum) with which torque is transmitted to the wire. These
should be checked for solidity and smooth operation if nothing else.
Whether there is enough suspicion to warrant taking the compass
off a binnacle stand or a panel off a powerboat's console is an on-
the-spot judgment. From past experience, I would not get excited
about clanking noises in these places until I was sure they weren't
due to slack in the wire, which would let the thimbles at the ends of
the chain slap the wall of the stand or console.

Propulsion gear, from the top: Fiberglass shaft log well tabbed to the hull, length of hose, stuffing box, shaft, and shaft coupling. Are there indications that the stuffing box has been weeping too freely? Is the set screw in the shaft coupling tight? Are those two seacocks to starboard turning freely? (May as well check them while we're here.) Are the seacocks and that through hull to port well bonded to the hull and free of corrosion?

Mechanical and hydraulic systems should share the same survey philosophy, though some of their problems differ from those of a wire system. Smooth, sure, powerful transmission of wheel motion to rudder, especially when the helm is reversed, is the foremost consideration. But, again, mechanical testing should be supplemented by a detailed inspection of the drive train for potential or developing problems. As a last resort, when operation leaves something to be desired but it would require playing the mechanic to delve into some part of the system, a surveyor can simply report his dissatisfaction and recommend that its source be investigated. It's sometimes hard for an old boatbuilder-surveyor to keep hands off intriguing problems that he is supposed to discover but not necessarily to analyze exhaustively, taking the boat apart in the process.

PROPELLER, SHAFT, STERN BEARING, STUFFING BOX

It is customary to record the diameter, pitch, and rotation (right- or left-hand) of a propeller, as well as its material, style, number of blades, and condition. It should be checked for a tight, secure fit on the shaft (you'd be surprised how many times the cotter pin is missing), cracks, pitting, and electrolytic attack as well as the usual nicks or bent blades. A propeller that's a poor match to the engine or hull should be remarked.

By rotating the propeller, one can sometimes actually see that a propeller shaft is bent. Shoving the shaft and propeller from side to side and up and down may cause a rattle in the stern bearing. Most often this signifies that the bearing is worn, but sometimes the shaft is worn, too. One should be careful that the shaft is not in gear, since it is possible to start up a diesel engine inadvertently. Neither is a rubber stern bearing helped by turning the shaft in it very much, even by hand, for the rubber needs water to lubricate it.

The propeller shaft should be examined for pitting and corrosion as well. One should also remember to look at the shaft inside the boat, its fit and how it is secured in the coupling. Without a set screw, which is sometimes left loose or unwired, a propeller and shaft have been known to screw themselves right out of the boat, as happened to one of my clients when he was backing down to set the anchor on his maiden cruise. Fortunately he was able to retrieve them and slide them back into place. It's just one more of the thousands of startling possibilities a surveyor ought to know about. Hopefully, most of them will be learned through vicarious rather than direct embarrassment.

Top: *A propeller, a shaft with two zincs, and a strut with an inserted rubber bearing. Always wiggle the shaft to see whether the bearing is worn, rotate the propeller to see whether the shaft is bent, check the tightness and cotter key of prop and nut, look for corrosion, note the condition of the zincs, and note the dimensions of shaft and prop.*

Bottom: *The zinc collar on this shaft is restricting the flow of lubricating water through the rubber stern bearing's lining. One-half shaft diameter is the "rule of thumb" minimum spacing between the zinc or propeller hub and the after end of the bearing.*

A flax-packed outside combination stern bearing/stuffing box, still a favorite where an inside stuffing box would be too difficult to service. It should last for years with only tightening and repacking.

By far the most popular bearing and stuffing box arrangement used on both sail and powerboats in this country today combines a rubber-lined bearing outboard at the sternpost or strut, just forward of the propeller, with a rubber-necked, flax-packed stuffing box on the interior. In a fiberglass boat, the hose neck of the stuffing box is usually clamped to a tubular, fiberglass shaft log, and very often the rubber bearing insert is pressed into the other end of the fiberglass tube and retained with set screws. Alternatively, a bronze casting containing a rubber bearing insert is bolted to the sternpost, as it is on wooden boats; hardly any glass-boat builders are unregenerate enough to cling to the bronze base for the inside stuffing box as well.

Rubber bearings and rubber-necked, flax-packed stuffing boxes are simple, straightforward pieces of hardware, easily serviced and

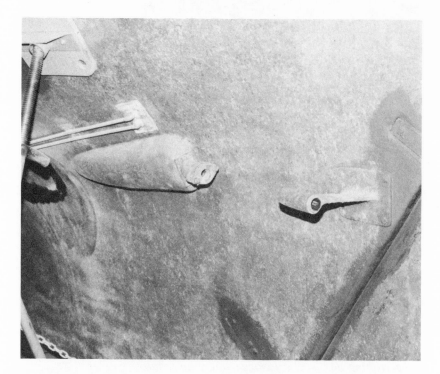

Still another arrangement, this one for an off-center propeller. Moving forward from just forward of the rudder, we see the strut with a rubber bearing insert, the outside, flax-packed stuffing box, and the shaft log. Just above that are outside pipes for an engine cooling system. By the way, the fiberglass covering on this wooden boat passes under all the hardware, as it should. (Courtesy Elen Boat Works)

easier to survey, except that stuffing boxes are often buried so deep in the recess of the hollow keel—behind the engine and under cockpit tubs, fuel tanks, and exhaust lines—that it is difficult just to get a look at them and all but impossible to get hands or wrenches on them. It's not surprising that the old saw, "It's best if stuffing boxes drip," has renewed popularity.

Some boats—especially powerboats with hollow Novie keels so long and deep that it is at best very inconvenient to reach an inside stuffing box—use a flax-packed stuffing box–stern bearing on the after side of the sternpost. One of these usually only needs tightening or repacking if the shaft is loose or leaking; it is a simple and inexpensive way of providing the functions of bearing and sealing. The more complicated division of the two functions has been brought on primarily by a preference for being able to work on the stuffing box inside the boat rather than having to haul her out or go swimming with a wrench, as some of us used to do occasionally.

Now and then one sees stern bearings with metal, wood, or plastic surfaces, which may be water lubricated, grease packed, or kept grease fed through remote grease cups. These are often foreign-built affairs, the most sophisticated I've seen being the Sabb feathering propeller and shaft unit with its integral, grease-filled stuffing box–stern bearing. Despite the fact that some of them require checking and servicing by mechanics, a surveyor can usually tell when a bearing is badly worn or something else is going sour and needs attention.

ENGINE

The following comments apply almost exclusively to inboard engines, for two reasons. First, in 40 years I haven't heard of one outboard-driven powerboat being surveyed, although that may change in these times of huge, expensive outboards driving big, sophisticated boats. Second, when surveying a boat that has an outboard motor for auxiliary power, most surveyors simply note its make, year, horsepower, and serial number; a meaningful assessment of mechanical condition requires testing by an outboard mechanic.

At the same time, a surveyor can and does check the soundness of the well or mounting bracket, availability of fresh air to the engine (some outboards in wells are so enclosed that they choke on the fumes from their exhaust-pressure relief port, which spews smoke out of the lower unit above water), and the safety of the fuel tank and its storage.

Admittedly, a surveyor's objection to judging the mechanical condition of outboard motors applies equally to the inner workings of inboard engines. I, for one, am willing to start and run an engine and to try the boat underway, but only as any reasonably experienced boatman can do—and in my case as a boatbuilder—not with any intention of analyzing the engine's performance. As far as I know, the majority of surveyors take a similar stand with engines, holding that for an in-depth study of an engine's condition the buyer should hire a practicing marine mechanic.

On the other hand, innumerable details related to the installation and maintenance of an inboard engine can be readily observed on its exterior, even when the boat is in storage, and should be studied as part of any survey. Many of these items are part of or associated with systems listed under other headings in the survey report, but they should be listed with the engine also because some parts of them can only be inspected while one is looking over the engine. Thus, after dutifully noting the size, make, fuel, number of cylinders, horsepower, model and serial number, type of cooling (fresh or raw water), and perhaps the gear reduction and gear used, one should give the engine and its accessory or satellite systems a thorough study, as follows:

● The propulsion gear from engine to stuffing box or shaft log, including gearbox and shift control, should be examined as described earlier.

● The cooling system, from raw water intake to the expulsion of same via exhaust, shaft log, or its own through hull, should be studied. Be there but a couple of small lines to and from a raw-water cooled engine in a small auxiliary or a busy network of strainers, heat exchangers, expansion tanks, valves, and hoses surrounding a powerboat's pair of huge diesels and auxiliary generator, it never ceases to astonish me what streaks, spatters, and rampant rust from water leaks are sometimes unnoticed or ignored. The source may be as trivial as a loose hose clamp, but the damage in the long run can be costly.

The engine in a boat laid up in a freezing climate should be checked to make sure that every part of the cooling system has been either drained or filled with antifreeze.

● The fuel system warrants close attention. The same dangers,

Coast Guard regulations, and insurer concerns that apply to fuel tanks and lines also apply to external filters and valves and to every part on the engine through which fuel passes, especially when it's gasoline. With diesel fuel, the surveyor worries mostly about leaks, including oil spurting from the high-pressure connections; with gasoline, not only leaks but such details as glass-bowl filters, carburetors other than down-draft, and the absence of flame arrestors raise his eyebrows.

• What about the lubricating oil? Is it leaking out of valve covers, gaskets, or shaft seals? Is there an effective oil pan? Is oil being thrown about the engine room? Are the bilges saturated with it? Is a large quantity of it floating on the bilge water?

Always a signal of engine trouble or bad housekeeping, oily bilges are a fire hazard, too. Since the Coast Guard and others have been tracking oil spills and prosecuting anyone responsible for discharging oil, a minor incident such as a boat beginning to flood while on its mooring can become a calamity if the bilge has oil in it. A surveyor should be quick to recommend that oil leaks be stopped and bilges cleaned.

• Check the electrical system. Every engine is squarely at the center of a boat's DC electrical system, and with electric starting and battery charging there are cables, wires, solenoids, starters, and generators or alternators, not to mention gauges, alarm senders, and a gasoline engine's ignition system, all of which deserve at least an inquiring look. A surveyor who does not undertake to analyze the engine can still do the buyer a great service if he will notice and report poor connections, badly run or physically unsuitable or deteriorated wiring, or water dripping down on or being thrown against electrical parts. The flywheel of an engine sitting low in a flooded bilge will pick up water with its ring gear teeth and throw it against the starter, ruining that expensive and at times desperately needed part.

The following excerpt from the survey of a 25-foot four-year-old single-screw speed boat shows what one might find, even when condition and maintenance seem almost perfect:

> The engine had clean oil, full; the bilge under it was clean; and there was antifreeze in the freshwater cooling system. Although the engine

looked very clean and well kept, there was some rust stain down over the forward end, rust on the alternator and its bracket, and a light stain showing that there had been some water slung against the engine bed by the belt or pulleys. The highest point and probable source of this water seemed to be the flange of the heat exchanger bolted on top of the engine, whose gasket we suspect of leaking. Whatever this small source, it should be found, and it would be good if, before the outdrive unit is reinstalled on the boat, the mechanic would start the engine and find this leak, and also check out the alternator, which could easily be in trouble from the water.

Sure enough, the alternator was, in fact, ruined, so that the price of the survey was retrieved through that one paragraph.

EXHAUST

This is both the last of the engine-related systems and the next subject I like to consider in my reports. For the half century that I have been aware of them, most exhaust systems in yachts have carried the gases to a through hull at the stern, cooling them along the way with exhausted cooling water. In the majority of shoal-hulled powerboats, where the top of the engine is well above the waterline, the system has always been quite simple. An elbow at the aft end of the manifold carries the gases down to a point where it is safe to inject the cooling water, and a steam hose or solid pipe carries the mixture to the stern. There may or may not be a muffler in the line. In some boats, the surveyor finds the elbow off the engine water jacketed and cool, while in others it is made up of heavy black iron pipe fittings and is run hot. Short-lived but cheap and easily replaced, the only concern with this hot section is how close it is to rusting out and whether it is likely to burn someone or something if not lagged with asbestos. Unfortunately, if it is well wrapped the surveyor can't tell its condition, but if it isn't, he may feel obliged to tell the buyer that it should be. Naturally, the hose, its clamps, which should be double (two on each connection), and the fitting through the stern should be checked for exhaust leaks, water leaks, or any signs of deterioration due to age.

A hot, dry exhaust elbow and union of iron pipe. A likely place to burn an arm.

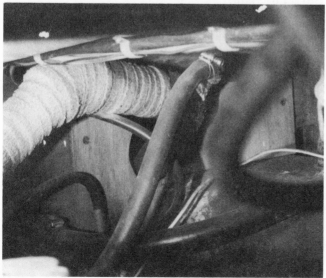

A "lagged" exhaust pipe.

Simple as these systems are, they can be an enigma loaded with potential trouble if there is a long, inaccessible run, perhaps down each side of a big twin-screw boat. The system, perhaps with a muffler and some metal or fiberglass sections clamped in along the line, may travel through several staterooms or compartments where it is buried under berths, lockers, and tanks. No hose lasts forever, and many an engine has been stifled by dislocated flaps of rubber obstructing the exhaust within a hose. Nobody likes to tear up the interior arrangement and pull the system apart to see how it's doing, so about all a surveyor can do is to get a look and a poke where possible, while judging mostly from external appearances.

It used to be that by far the best exhaust system one could have was one water jacketed all the way from engine to stern, with the water switching from the jacket to the interior just before the through hull. The engine can be below the waterline as long as a loop of the line is carried well above it at some point between engine and through hull. In older wooden boats and many of the earlier fiberglass boats, one still sees the curved, double-walled, all-copper systems shaped and brazed together by specialty shops. There was a chap named "Louie" Schwab from Providence, Rhode Island, who would climb into a boat with a piece of stiff wire once the engine was on its beds, bend the wire this way and that, take a few measurements, and bring you back a gleaming work of copper-smithery that fitted just right.

Water-jacketed copper exhausts were a joy—that's my eulogy on them. But they were never cheap, and diesel exhaust is said to be dangerous to their health; two generations of simpler, lightweight systems have supplanted them for use with engines below the waterline as well as above. First came the stack systems. These use various configurations of exhaust line and water jacketing to get the gases up to the needed height above the waterline, after which gases combine with cooling water and flow aft. In a typical example, exhaust gases travel up the inside pipe of a double-walled stack, exit into the outside pipe from under an umbrella on top of which the cooling water is sprayed, and the mixture of gases and water goes down between the pipes, through the wall of the outside pipe into a nipple, and then aft in a steam hose. Many of these stacks, welded up in copper for gasoline engines or in stainless steel for diesels, are

Looking aft at an engine with stack-type exhaust. To starboard (on the left) is a heat exchanger. To port is the stack. The small pipe carries cooling water to the top of the stack, where it sprays down over an umbrella. The central conduit of the stack carries gases up under the umbrella, and the cooled gases sink in the stack's outer conduit and are then carried aft.

still in service in older boats. As long as they reach a height unassailable by surges from following seas and pitching, they protect the engine perfectly from flooding.

The latest system, used with 90 percent of all new boats with engines below the waterline, is the waterlift muffler exhaust line. As described in Chapter 3, the waterlift system's main advantages are utter simplicity and economy, and there is considerable flexibility in the placement of the high loop. Adapting the system to work with

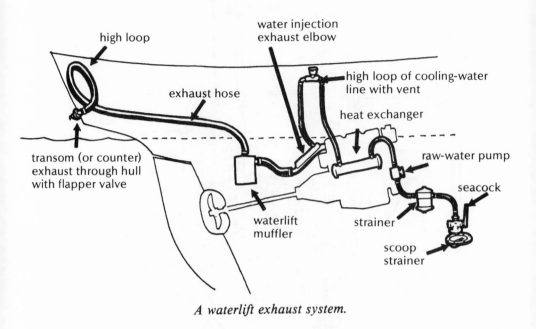

A waterlift exhaust system.

below-the-waterline engines adds but one major part, a cannister-muffler to collect any water left in the line between engine and loop when the engine shuts down. The idea that cooling water injected into the exhaust line just abaft the engine could be blown over a high loop and out aft without any of it backing into the engine was a daring one. The cannister placed well below the engine as a reservoir is essential, and so is a siphon break in a high loop of the cooling water line; otherwise, the entire system—cannister, engine and all—could be quietly flooded after being shut down. As a surveyor, I remain uneasy about one of these systems until I have laid eyes on a loop of the cooling water line that is carried to the necessary height and provided with either a small air valve or a narrow tube communicating with the exhaust's high loop (the latter being the more failsafe system where practicable). I might also point out that one could conceivably flood a waterlift system by cranking and cranking on a hard-starting engine with a good raw water pump; cooling water would be pumped into the exhaust line during the cranking, and there would be no engine exhaust to blow it out.

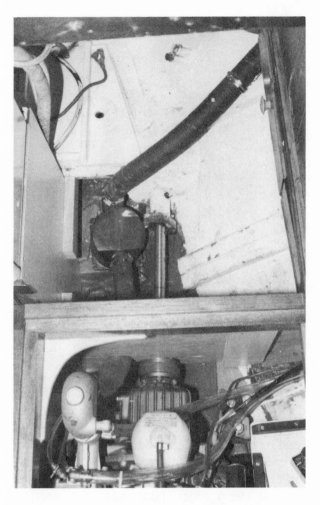

Looking down on an engine with waterlift muffler. At extreme bottom of photograph, cooling water leaves the engine's heat exchanger and is carried up to port through the clear-walled hose to a high loop (out of view). The hose reenters the picture and leads back down to the engine, where it connects to a high elbow off the exhaust manifold. Here the cooling water is injected into the exhaust, and the mixture is carried down through the heavy exhaust hose to the muffler or "pot" (center of photo). From there the exhaust line leads aft and upward, through a high loop (off the top righthand corner of the photo), and finally to a through hull in the counter. (Courtesy Elen Boat Works)

The cooling-water intake seacock and strainer. The surveyor's big beef with seacocks is that they are seldom used, almost always frozen with corrosion, and almost never cleaned and greased.

In any of these systems, the surveyor is looking for leaks, corrosion, cracked metal, rusted clamps, loose or deteriorated hose, or a loose through hull. It is crucial that water jackets, stacks, and cannisters be drained or have antifreeze added when systems are laid up for winter.

Other details worth noting are hoses collapsed at too-tight bends or from bearing against sharp edges, poor support of sections suspended from the overhead, spatial conflicts with the moving parts of steerers or engine controls, and the likelihood of damage from heavy gear stowed near the exhaust line.

FUEL SYSTEMS

Until about 20 years ago, gruesome casualties due to gasoline fires and explosions were an expanding aspect of the yachting scene.

Since then, the toll has drastically diminished despite a multimillion boat increase in the fleet. Three factors contributed to the improvement: increased public awareness of how deadly gasoline fumes in a boat can be, stringent Coast Guard regulations concerning gasoline fuel systems installed by yacht builders*, and a widespread switch to diesel power.

Because of the history, the regulations, the anxiety of insurers, and the threat to the buyer's or owner's safety, the surveyor must be on the alert for every sign of danger, present or potential, in a gasoline fuel system. Naturally, he makes an essentially parallel search for problems in a diesel system; although it is much less volatile and as yet unregulated, nobody wants diesel fuel loose in a boat, either. The following is a list of positive and negative characteristics a surveyor looks for in a fuel system:

1) Leaks in the tank.

2) Rust or corrosion on the tank.

3) Fittings or connections anywhere except the top surface of the tank. All other locations are illegal with gasoline, handy though they are for draining or flushing the tank.

4) Blocking, chocks, strapping, fiberglass tabbing, or some combination of these to keep the tank from moving in any direction. (Integral tanks are illegal for gasoline.)

5) Electrical grounding of the deck fill plate to the tank and of tank to engine and keel bolts or "bonding system." Grounding is mandatory for gasoline systems because it keeps static electricity from building up to a spark and a you-know-what.

6) Location of the deck fill plate. The weather deck is best. It is illegal to locate a gasoline fill plate where the gasoline or its fumes can get below.

The regulations referred to in this and the following sections are set forth in the Coast Guard's book Rules and Regulations for Recreational Boating. *Additional insights into safe and proper engine, fuel, heating, electrical, and other systems for small boats are provided in the American Boat and Yacht Council's* Standards and Recommended Practices for Small Craft, *available from the ABYC, P. O. Box 806, 190 Ketcham Ave., Amityville, NY 11701.*

The top of a fuel tank and underside of the deck showing the fill, with the deck-plate hose sloping down from left to right to connect to the tank fitting; the grounding wire from the tank to the deck plate; the vent (lower left) with hose running to vent fitting topside; the vent cap, which can be removed in order to "stick" the tank; and the supply line, with a shut-off valve at the tank.

The deck plate must be tight to the deck, and the hose between it and the tank must also be tight, lest fuel leak belowdeck. A solid pipe (with no hose section) from deck to tank is frowned upon, because its rigidity might cause the plate to break loose from the deck, or the tank fitting to break loose from the tank, or the top of the tank to crack given motion of the deck or tank relative to each other. Such motion is more a probability than a possibility in a fiberglass boat.

7) Location of the fuel vent. The vent should not be placed where it might take in water or, if the system is overfilled, where it will spew out fuel that runs into the boat. Such a location would, again, be illegal with gasoline. A flame arrestor screen is mandatory on a gasoline tank vent, by the way.

Typical locations of vents are on the transom or topsides aft, just below the deck edge or guard rail, or on the outboard face of the

An exhaust blower in 4-inch vacuum-type hose.

cockpit coamings or house sides. None of these locations is universally safe from a dousing in rough going. Recently, I found the fuel vent of a William Hand motorsailer seven feet above the cockpit sole, in the after face of one of the posts holding up her shelter top. Its copper tubing ran up the inside of the post from belowdeck. Across a half century I silently saluted the able Mr. Hand for the most ingenious fuel vent installation I'd ever seen.

8) The fuel supply line. A shutoff at the tank; a siphon break; a fuel pump that doesn't leak if its diaphragm is ruptured; Coast Guard type "A" and "B" hose; hose fittings with a flare, annular ridges, or serrations; clamps that do not depend on spring tension and do not cut the hose; filter/separators that don't have glass bowls and are supported in place by means other than hanging in the fuel line; fuel lines that are themselves fastened at regular intervals; a flexible section of fuel line between any rigid tubing or piping and the engine; and much, much more is mandated or desirable, with a different degree of urgency or the force of law depending on whether the fuel is gasoline or diesel. If the past is any indication, there will be more industry standards and regulations before there are fewer.

Either the manufacturer or some subsequent repairer is responsible for having installed the fuel system according to regulations. At the same time, not one surveyor I know is so cavalier as not to mention that a detail is illegal, for it is the only way to save the buyer, owner, or insurer from possible future hassles or worse.

9) Ventilation. When gasoline is the fuel, there are Coast Guard regulations spelling out the requirements for ventilation. In the 1960s, when the law first became effective, hundreds of thousands if not millions of boats were suddenly required to install additional ventilation to the engine and tank spaces. To meet the deadline, boatshops such as mine with a capability to make small fiberglass parts, as well as rubber product manufacturers and vendors, were kept busy day and night for several months supplying fiberglass cowels and 4-inch vacuum-type hoses. Unless somebody was exaggerating the situation, there should have been a precipitous drop in boating fires and explosions at that time.

In these calmer times, the manufacturer of the boat is primarily responsible for compliance. Nevertheless, the surveyor should look over the ventilation system and note the number of cowels and trunks (boxes or ducts between the cowels and belowdeck areas), where the latter terminate below, and if and where there is a blower. His report will then bear witness to the legality of a gasoline system or the adequacy of a diesel installation. The rest is up to the recipient of the survey.

Perhaps because no law applies to the ventilation of diesel-powered boats, I have twice found that a builder provided not one tiny hole into the engine and tank space to bring fresh air to a diesel engine. Both boats were small auxiliaries, and their little engines were surviving on air that leaked in under cockpit seat locker hatches, around access doors belowdeck, and through such things as the slot for a bilge pump handle. As any mechanic will tell you, diesels gulp a lot of air and put out a lot of heat, and a space that tight amounts to an inefficient installation to say the least. A builder may wish to protect a diesel from any salt water coming on deck, but he should nevertheless provide a snorkel for aspiration, its diameter being somewhat greater than that of the engine's air intake.

BATTERY

Some people, including some fiberglass boat manufacturers, don't seem to realize that batteries can be dangerous. Not only does battery acid dissolve one's clothing or any other organic material (including skin), but the hydrogen a battery releases while being charged will explode readily given the smallest spark, possibly showering a person with acid and burning him badly. A more constant danger is the likelihood of a short circuit caused by metal objects bridging the terminals of an uncovered battery. The resultant red-hot heating of the connecting metal and ignition of any nearby inflammable materials is a not-so-nice prospect.

Vaporproof master battery off/on or selector switches are mandatory with gasoline fuel systems, for many people have blown themselves out of a boat in the act of turning on its power when gasoline fumes—or liquefied petroleum gas (LPG)—lurked below. By far the most common fault I have found with battery installations in all sorts of boats is a tendency not to secure them well, either with a deep-sided battery box or with hold-down straps or bands, to keep them from tumbling over in a seaway.

WIRING

Everyone knows that the insulation on boat wiring should meet the industry standards, which vary according to its use in the boat and whether the associated electric potential is above or below 50 volts. Most of us know also that because prolonged vibration eventually "hardens" single wires, they should, generally, be stranded. Less well understood is the fact that relatively large wire sizes are needed for the low voltages, long runs, and, at times, heavy currents involved in shipboard electrical systems.

Not every surveyor is an electrician, but he can usually tell a good wiring job from a poor one; he can spot skinny wires, wires likely to be overloaded, and those that are poorly supported, badly connected, or not well-enough insulated where connected.

In many cases the wire itself is satisfactory, but receptacles and plugs, light sockets, and other components are defective. When built for shoreside use, these are often of flimsy plastic construction that can't stand hard use; worse, they often contain steel parts that disintegrate quickly in the marine environment.

There are regulations pertaining to wiring, connections, and spark-producing components in gasoline-powered boats. None are so onerous that I would mind following them in a diesel boat as well, and that's saying something, for the very word "regulation" tends to make me stubborn and willful if not downright unreasonable.

FUSES AND SWITCHES

Fuses and switches, automatic and manual, keep an electrical system under control. They are used to avert the sometimes disastrous consequences of overloads and short circuits, and they permit work on defective circuits while others continue to serve the boat. Today, most installations employ circuit breakers, which function both as switches and resettable fuses. The job is perfectly well done by separate switches and fuses, and has been for about a century, but it's less convenient to replace a fuse than it is to snap a circuit breaker back on when an overload has been corrected.

Now and then the surveyor will find a switch panel, a terminal strip, or a row of fuses so located that it is getting wet. On a powerboat this could be due to a pilothouse window leak; on a small auxiliary, the panel might be mounted over a hole in the main bulkhead so that its wiring and connections are exposed in a dank engine space or seat locker. Although the obvious recommendation for deck or hatch leaks is that they be fixed, it is also worthwhile to recommend that a removable, protective cover be fitted over connections sharing a locker with such well-salted items as fenders, lines, sailbags, and mops.

AUXILIARY GENERATOR

No matter the kind or size of generator set, the problems its engine might develop are too nearly identical to those of propulsion engines to restudy here. As with the main engine, a surveyor who isn't a mechanic will confine himself to assessing its installation and external systems. If he also isn't much of an electrician, he will confine his study of that part of the set to its external physical condition, the wiring, connections, fuses, and switches. If that sounds like a waste of time, I can only say, "You never know."

Sent to do an insurance update on a big old twin-screw

powerboat, I was having my usual mild attack of feeling superfluous as I pulled up the rug and hatches of her spacious deck salon, hopped down between two giant engines, and plodded through an examination of the intricate pipe, tubing, hose, cable, and wire systems around me. Over in the corner was a new generator set, installed the year before. Because it was larger than the old set, the location had been moved, I could see, from a bed between the engines where I was standing. In fact, here was an abandoned power cable to the former set, still dangling from a stringer. I pulled it out of the bilge and found that the end of it was a brilliant green plume of verdigris. When you see that on copper wire in a boat, it's more likely to be electrolytic action than simple corrosion. I traced the cable back to the AC distribution panel and couldn't believe where it ended: still tied into the main fuses, alive as anything when the set was on. When I expressed my incredulity, the insurer's representative said, "That's why we sent you. You never know."

SHORE POWER

More and more boats, even some of the tiniest "two sleepers," are equipped with shore power today. As new marinas are built and fill up instantly, their new customers are plugging in. And why not, when with shore power they can live aboard at the marina with all the conveniences of a cottage by the sea, keep the boat's DC system charged up, and even work aboard with AC power tools?

Why not indeed, except that everything has its price, and part of the price of shore power is increased danger to people on the boat. Two factors work to increase the danger of electric utility AC power when it is brought aboard: First, dampness—made more pervasive by the salt in ocean water—increases the electrical conductivity of everything on a boat, including people. The dampness means a greater likelihood of "stray" currents aboard than ashore, and a more severe shock or burn as the consequence of tangling with one of these.

Second, one "side" or wire of the pair in every 110 volt electric utility circuit is grounded. There is also a potential of 110 volts between each wire of a 220 volt circuit and ground, because the 220 volt secondary coil of the power transformer is center tapped, and the center tap is grounded. The resultant configuration is the familiar 110/220 volt three-wire service, with 220 volts between the two ungrounded wires and 110 volts between the grounded wire and each of the other two. Grounding is an important safety feature ashore, but the service into a house is permanent, not plugged in at the dock. Without proper shore power cables and plugs and receptacles that can't be reversed, there's a 50-50 chance that a boat will be plugged in backward, sending the "hot" side of the power through the grounded side of the boat's circuits. When that happens, any fixture or appliance aboard is live; danger to people is increased many fold, and problems with the boat itself, ranging from electrical fires to destruction of metal parts by electrolysis, may result.

In studying the boat's shore power system, the surveyor should note and report whether it has irreversible plugs and receptacles. At the same time, because this safeguard can be circumvented by the use of pigtails with ordinary two-prong plugs on one end and the special three-prong plugs on the other, many boats' shore power systems are provided with a polarity indicator that will sound an alarm if the incoming current's polarity is reversed. This is an important safety feature when the system is a grounded one.

Working on the principle that grounded electric utility power is more a liability than an asset aboard a boat, some boats are equipped with what is called an isolation transformer. Shore power is fed into the primary coil of a transformer, and the ship's power is taken off the secondary coil (not connected to the primary in any way) and is kept "floating," or clear of any connection with ground throughout the boat. Such a system is considered safer than electric utility power because the wires in each circuit are "hot" relative only to each other; neither is hot relative to ground. Nevertheless, this safeguard, too, has been rendered worthless by people who didn't think or didn't know about what they were doing. I got a call one morning from an owner whose daughter had gotten a jolt from a toaster that was on shore power in their boat's galley. Checking the toaster and a number of other points in the 110 volt circuitry with his meter, he found a potential of 40 to 80 volts between these points and such "grounds" as the water system, the stainless steel sink, counter tops, and even the propane gas stove. "Of course," he agreed, "the metal case of the toaster should be insulated from the 110 volt circuitry. But even though it obviously isn't, how could there be a potential between the 110 and ground when it comes 'floating' from an isolation transformer in the engine room?"

An investigation of the boat's electrical system turned up a rather special reason for the problem: Someone in the past who wanted 220 volts as well as 110 volts throughout the boat had bypassed the isolation transformer with the 220 volt circuitry, the transformer not being able to handle both. Whoever it was had then run the 220 volts and the transformer's output of isolated 110 volts around the boat in three wires, both voltages sharing one of them. Since that time, it seems, the isolation transformer had just been going along for the ride.

Switching from the big picture to the little things, there is a natural tendency to use inexpensive and easily obtained electrical fixtures made for house and camper use, but these must be watched for steel parts that disintegrate rapidly into rust. I have sometimes had the "innards" of light fixtures fall apart in my hands, and have often seen fixtures that were abandoned because rust got the better of them.

THROUGH HULLS AND SEACOCKS

If there is not going to be a seacock on it, the most troublefree, durable, and economical through hull in a fiberglass hull is one formed by glassing a fiberglass tube to the hull. Such an assembly becomes a part of the hull and should last just about as long. The surveyor should inspect the fiberglass attachment and the hose that is usually clamped onto the inboard end.

When a through hull requires pipe threads onto which a seacock or valve can be screwed, nothing (yet) beats the traditional choice of bronze. Delrin through hulls are lighter, cheaper, and not subject to corrosion or electrolytic destruction, but they can be broken or cracked far more easily than bronze. For the past 20 years, a number of builders have solved that dilemma by using Delrin above the waterline and bronze below it. The surveyor should examine a threaded through hull for watertightness where clamped to the hull, physical defects, electrolysis (if it's bronze), and, while he's at it, for fouling. Marine organisms such as barnacles can plug up a through hull entirely, especially those intake through hulls that are covered by strainers, which inhibit the application of antifouling paint within.

There are, of course, several other types of through hulls, ranging in size from relatively tiny fuel tank vents to cavernous exhaust outlets. Partly because they have a flame arresting screen built in—to meet regulations for gasoline tank installations—cast vents with threaded bodies and downward-looking openings in their pillbox-shaped heads seem to be the most common ones today. In simpler times, we just brought out a copper tube and made it look downward so that it wouldn't ingest rain or spray, or flared it at the surface and covered it with a small cowel. The copper tube is still legal for diesel fuel, but not for gasoline unless you take the trouble to fit a piece of wire screen over the opening. Ah well, the cast ones are quite solid and durable in chrome-plated bronze, and have given no trouble that I know of, except that once in a great while I find one from which the hose or copper tubing has become disconnected. Then too, I once found bees living in a vent that had no screen.

Most engine exhausts today find their way into steam hose, even if it is but a short length to make a vibration-expansion joint between a through hull and a metal—or, today, fiberglass—line. Exhaust through hulls, therefore, are almost all designed to take a hose. Essentially a tube with integral flange that is bolted to the hull or transom, an exhaust through hull may be cast bronze, or copper, or cupronickel, or stainless tubing with the flange welded on, or merely a fiberglass tube glassed to a fiberglass hull. The common problems are loosened attachment to the hull, a loose connection of the hose, or hose clamps that are broken or so badly rusted that they will soon be broken. Indeed, hose clamps not made entirely of stainless steel often find their way aboard boats, where their plain steel parts don't last long.

Bronze depthsounder transducers that fit up to the hull or to a fairing block and are clamped there by a nut on their threaded stems never seem to give much trouble, and that is fortunate, for I see more and more of these abandoned in favor of a new transducer for a new depthsounder. At best this practice is not very neat, and I always mention it in the hope that someone will be moved to take out the old transducer and patch the hole. "The fewer through hulls the better," is a good slogan; many sailboat transducers are now fitted to the inside of the hull within a canister of water, and the signal seems to pass through the fiberglass skin well enough.

In the traditional seacock installation, the threaded body of the through hull screws directly into the base of the seacock so that the skin of the hull is clamped between their flanges. The old tapered-barrel seacock with ample base or flange is a fine piece of hardware. Built of heavy bronze, it is good for the life of at least one boat, barring a terminal attack of electrolytic corrosion. If it is kept greased and used regularly, it will rarely develop any problem, but if it is unused and unserviced for years on end, it will freeze, and will not budge until it is taken apart and cleaned up.

Cleaning and greasing the seacocks used to be a regular part of the maintenance of any boat hauled and stored in a boatyard, but today, only a few yards catering to the "carriage trade" dare do such work without a specific work order. It being the nature of most yachtsmen never to touch a seacock unless it is absolutely necessary, it is a rare survey that does not turn up seacocks that are "frozen" or heavily coated with corrosion from weeping.

Much the same fate befalls bronze gate valves, which are often substituted for seacocks to save money. Unfortunately, gate valves are too delicate internally to survive being forced open or shut when they bind up with corrosion, and they invariably become scrap metal when not kept free with frequent use. Only this spring I tried to turn the handle of a gate valve in a cockpit drain line and snapped it. The interesting part of that episode was that the valve was stuck closed, meaning apparently that the owner didn't know his cockpit had had only one working drain for an unknown number of months or years.

When it is fairly certain, and it usually is today, that seacocks or gate valves will be neglected and are likely to be frozen when needed, ball valves would be preferable. A bronze-bodied ball valve with a stainless steel ball in a nylon seat will go a very long time with no use at all in salt water and still operate easily. I don't know any statistics, but I have yet to find one that was inoperable. Donald Street once made the statement that they had been known to go 10 years without attention and still turn freely. At the same time, I have found some of them equipped with steel handles that would rust to pieces a lot sooner than that, and I have heard of others with interior works held in place by a brass nut, which could conceivably "dezincify" and let the whole assembly fall apart. Those are things to watch out for, but when it comes to troublefree operation, I'd rather have bronze, stainless, and nylon ball valves than any other kind of seacock. They also happen to be cheaper by far than traditional seacocks, though I hate to mention that lest some people relate low cost to inferiority.

In any case, the surveyor's job is to try each handle and examine every seacock, and to note those that are frozen and those with leaks, signs of corrosive disintegration, or other problems.

BILGE PUMPS

The greatest number of bilge pumps I have seen on one boat is nine. They were Lovett electric submersibles scattered along the bottom of an older 65-foot twin-screw motorboat, which had splits in her double fore-and-aft planking in way of innumerable broken ribs on both sides. Somehow, she made a trip from Florida to Essex, Connecticut, with her gang of pumps and canvas patches on both sides.

I begin to suspect copious leaking when there is more than one electric pump in a boat whose bilge has only one definite low point, or more than two electric pumps in, say, a motorboat that changes her trim while underway, so that she needs a pump forward when at rest and one aft when running. Electric pumps, almost exclusively, tell the story, for few owners today have time to tend a leaky boat with a hand pump. Carried a step further, it follows that pumps that battle a generous, constant leak will have automatic switches, while pumps in boats that leak only when underway, if at all, can have manual switches. Many an owner has taken out an automatic switch after it stuck in the "on" position and either ran the battery down or burned out the motor, but if the boat leaks badly enough, taking out the automatic switch is not an option.

I wouldn't overemphasize the importance of the number and type of pumps. It's just another clue to understanding a boat. Meanwhile, another potential concern with a permanently installed bilge pump is the danger of it siphoning water back into the boat. The most failsafe way to guard against this is to place the pump's exhaust through hull well above the waterline. This gets a bit tricky in a sailboat's topsides, which are sometimes rail down for hours on end and would require a siphon break, a check valve, or a large printed reminder close by the pump switch or handle to open and close a hand valve whenever the pump is operated. But it finally dawned on someone through the years that the transom of a sailboat is rarely underwater, and then not for long, and almost all sailboats now carry the pump's exhaust to the transom.

By far the most popular hand pump today, and with good reason, is the diaphragm type, taking the place of the bronze-barrel "Navy" type so popular several decades ago. The diaphragm type never needs priming, and it will pass considerable debris through its large "flap" valves, along with the most water per inch-pound of stroke that I know of. It is also the most easily cleaned, repaired, or rebuilt pump, requiring nothing more than a screwdriver and a small wrench or pair of pliers in most cases.

If a boat should be holed, or if a large underwater part should open up, high-capacity pumps, belt-driven by the engine's power takeoff, can avert a disastrous flooding. The presence of such a pump installation, and its capacity if known, certainly deserve mention in the survey report; it is a feature indicative of a determination to make the boat safer.

On the other hand, it is not the surveyor's job to make pronouncements about what pumps a boat should have. He should list the pumps it has, describe any that are of an uncommon variety or that are installed in an unusual way, note any existing or imminent malfunctions, and recommend suitable repairs. Provided with that information, it is up to the concerned party to decide whether the pumps and their condition are suitable to the boat and its projected use.

STOVES AND HEATERS

The surveyor's main concern with stoves and heaters is safety. Listed in ascending order of dangerousness, the most common fuels are electricity, solid fuels (wood, coal, charcoal), alcohol, kerosene and diesel fuel, CNG (compressed natural gas), LPG (liquefied petroleum gas), and gasoline.

The potential dangers of electricity are, of course, shock and fires started by overheated wiring. These are combated by appropriate wiring and fuses or breakers. While only larger boats with an auxiliary generator and shore power can have an electric cook stove or heater, I cannot remember a single incident of damage or personal injury caused by one. Thus, I associate electric stoves and heaters with maximum safety despite my remarks a few pages back

Despite the fan to the cockpit and the metal lining on the underside of the bridge deck, this stove is awfully close to the overhead.

about the danger associated with electric utility power or grounded systems aboard boats. A surveyor should look for clean, neat, and well-run and insulated wiring and electrical fixtures, a polarity indicator or isolation transformer on an incoming shore line, and proper fuses or breakers.

The worst threat of solid-fuel stoves and heaters is that a roaring fire will heat the stove or chimney hotter than the kindling point of wood or other materials close by. It behooves the surveyor, therefore, to look at the stove as if it were red hot and to consider whether the air space, insulation, surrounding metal, or the combination of these provides adequate shielding of adjacent flammable materials.

Of course, there is also a danger that very hot parts such as iron lids might be flung about the cabin by violent motion, or even that the fire itself could be dumped out in a severe knockdown. Except to note whether the stove itself is well lashed down, and if not, to recommend that it should be, most surveyors don't comment on such dangers.

Some people are sure to disagree with my opinion that alcohol is safer than the petroleum oils and the gases, and it is true that differences in the way stoves work can make one kind safer than another though it uses a more dangerous fuel. Nevertheless, burning alcohol can be extinguished with water, and there's no way one can run out of that on a boat.

Innumerable types of kerosene and fuel-oil boat stoves and heaters have been devised over the years, based on wicks, carburetion, pressurization, preheaters, and gun-type burners. Regardless of the type of burner, the most feared accident is flooding and the sudden ignition of a free puddle of oil. But if the prospect of burning oil is frightening, only terror can describe the prospect of a gas explosion on a boat, once one has experienced or has seen the results of one. LPG and gasoline fumes, being heavier than air, collect in a boat hull as though it were a bowl, ready to blow it apart at the least spark; there is no ignoring the danger.

The surveyor's job, then, is to worry about leaks associated with an oil-burning stove's supply lines and connections, and about faulty burners. He should look over the installation of LPG tanks and their lines and connections with this question uppermost in his

The right way: a cabin heater spaced away from the bulkhead, a heat deflector at its top, and the pipe also led away from the bulk-head. (Courtesy Elen Boat Works)

mind: Is there any way that escaped gas could get below and collect in the boat? A safe built-in locker for LPG gas bottles is one that is gas tight when its cover is closed, and it must have a drain through the topsides to let leaking gas go overboard. It is acceptable to put gas bottles in a deck box on a weather deck, providing the box with scuppers to let leaking gas out. As a last resort, the bottle in use as well as the spares can be kept right out in the open air on deck. I've seen them in racks on trunk tops, or on after decks lashed to a stanchion. Anything is better than belowdeck storage. The shutoff valve in the supply line should ideally be placed outside the hull or deck. That way there is no chance of gas leaking into the interior from the stove or line when the stove is not in use. A red light that goes on when the gas is turned on and a sniffer to warn of gas collecting in the bilge at any time are good news to insurers, too.

A seemingly innocent but potentially disastrous use of LPG aboard a boat is in the little propane camping stoves fueled by small "plug-in" tanks or canisters of gas. In startling conformity to Murphy's law, spare canisters stowed aboard boats have rusted through and, at some random moment, flooded the bilges with LPG. I don't know how other surveyors react, but the moment I see or hear of a portable LPG stove on a boat, I start protesting and lecturing.

Relief from the hazards of LPG comes in the form of CNG. Compressed natural gas is lighter than air, which makes it radically safer than any heavier-than-air gas or fumes; it will try to float up and out of a boat rather than settling into it. The nature of a boat being what it is, there's almost always an opening topside through which CNG can escape. Naturally, it's better to stow CNG tanks in a deck locker, which needs only a gap or vent near its top.

Without question, in my mind, gasoline is the most dangerous of all boat stove and heater fuels. Fortunately, its use is now rare.

REFRIGERATION AND AIR CONDITIONING

The majority of yachts under 35 feet still have iceboxes. This is hardly surprising, since they are sailed mostly on weekends, and a single loading of ice, surrounded with the insulation we now have, will last longer than it is needed. In fiberglass boats the surveyor is spared any worry about rot under the icebox, and even the drain or sump arrangement for meltwater is of reduced importance, because so much ice is now brought aboard in plastic bags or manufactured at home in plastic jugs. By freezing drinking water or any water-base drinks to take the place of ice, space is saved and meltwater eliminated. Nevertheless, if there is a drain to a through hull, a sump, or a sump pump, the surveyor should look them over for soundness and potential problems.

Except for obvious external problems, the average surveyor is unable to delve into the condition of any of the numerous boat refrigeration and freezer systems, which range from self-contained boxes to remote electric and engine-driven units used to cool built-in boxes. Neither is he likely to have more than a passing acquaintance with air conditioning. Nevertheless, there should be an inspection for obvious external problems or potential problems and an accurate description of the boat's system—be it a "mini-fridge" or enough machinery to cool an air-conditioned fish market—if only for the benefit of insurers and lenders.

FIRE EXTINGUISHERS

Few other pieces of equipment are as important to safety on a boat, especially one that carries highly flammable fuel, as a fire extinguisher. Indeed, the prudent owner carries more than one extinguisher, and he takes pains to install them so that there will be one readily available no matter where a fire might break out or where crew members might be when it does.

Cured polyester resin will not ignite until its temperature reaches 800 to 900 degrees Fahrenheit, or about twice the kindling point of wood, and I have seen the wooden joinerwork in a boat completely destroyed by fire without her fiberglass hull and deck burning at all. But one certainly can't plan on a low-temperature fire, and it is an ugly, dangerous matter when a laminate does reach its kindling point. The resin burns savagely, gives off a noxious smoke, and leaves nothing but limp sheets of fiberglass where there was once a structure. Once the resin ignites, immediate attack with a fire extinguisher or two could be the only hope of averting a total loss.

On today's small and medium size yachts, pressurized dry chemical extinguishers are common, being very cheap, readily available, and fairly effective, although rather messy in some instances because of the powder residue they leave. Carbon dioxide extinguishers are another strong favorite, and the newer Halon gas extinguishers are promising even better results.

For many years, the deluxe answer to the fire fighting problem on boats has been the permanently installed pressurized vapor system based on a large tank of CO_2, or, lately, of Halon gases, the gas being discharged manually or automatically into the engine-tank space in enough volume to snuff out a conflagration there. These are a great comfort to the yacht owner, and when properly set up, they can be used for more than one blast or firing of the gas to put out a flashback fire. The main difference between the CO_2 and the American Safety Products' Halonite is in the amount of oxygen they leave for people who happen to be in the blanketed area. CO_2 smothers the fire (and any people who remain in the area) by excluding any oxygen from it. Halonite's reaction is chemical, and there is still oxygen in the area to breathe while the fire is extinguished. The automatic systems are highly regarded by insurance companies for obvious reasons.

Because of the insurers' understandably intense interest in fire fighting equipment, the surveyor should be careful to describe in detail each extinguisher, to state whether or not it is charged, and to note which of the three classes of burning materials or fires its contents are supposed to extinguish: Class A—trash, paper, and wood products; Class B—flammable liquids; or Class C—electrical.

GROUND TACKLE

In contrast to fire extinguishers, I cannot remember much interest on the part of insurance companies in a boat's ground tackle. Interest in her permanent mooring, sometimes (especially in its location), but not in anchors and rodes. I don't know why, for I have always considered this gear a most important part of a boat's equipment. Indeed, I am often bold enough to recommend additions to and replacements of ground tackle, although that is not friendly ground. Few subjects in yachting are fraught with more personal preference and prejudice than the choice of anchors. Fortunately, the reader is spared discussion of the types and weights here, since it is a matter well covered in other literature.*

For example, Chapman, Charles F., et al. Piloting, Seamanship and Small Boat Handling. *56th ed. New York: Hearst, 1983.*

In my opinion, a surveyor should study and report on a boat's ground tackle. Further, he should be very critical of the deck hardware, including chocks, hawseholes or hawsepipes, cleats, bitts, and winches. Anything related to anchoring, mooring, or tying up the boat is important to her safety in the long view.

Unfortunately, thousands upon thousands of fiberglass production boats, especially those under 35 feet, are fitted out with undersized cleats and chocks. Builders and buyers apparently believe that these boats will always be tied up in sheltered marinas or anchored in quiet backwaters, and strong chocks and cleats would be an unnecessary expense. I must admit that I have surveyed many 5- to 10-year-old boats still getting by with ridiculously tiny original chocks and cleats. Often, pieces of this hardware, which I would be ashamed to use on a dinghy, are hanging loose, broken, or missing, and it doesn't seem to have bothered the owner at all. But as one who has seen innumerable boats of all types and sizes go ashore, and has known chocks and cleats to rip out of decks and decks to rip out of boats, too, I believe that the hardware for anchoring, towing, or tying up any boat should be just as strong and well fastened and its strains spread just as widely over the structure as possible.

SAFETY AND LIFESAVING

Under this heading I list features and gear of the boat that contribute to the crew's safety and survival—anything oriented toward avoiding injury or drowning. At the same time, I believe that the surveyor should not be expected to list every boathook, whistle, or PFD (personal flotation device), some of which may be stored in several places aboard or in the owner's beach house or garage. This is a task for the owner if the boat is being insured or for the broker if the boat is being sold. The surveyor has enough to worry about without taking inventory.

Typical safety and lifesaving items include a tender, life raft, lifelines, bow and stern rails, grab rails, safety harnesses, throwable life rings and horseshoes, swim ladder, stern platform or steps, man overboard buoys, lights, EPIRB (emergency position-indicating radio beacon), VHF radio, CB radio, flares, horn, whistle, bell, signal lights or flags, riding or anchor lights, spreader or other deck lights, searchlights, and strobe light.

DECK HARDWARE

Here again, there is not much reason for the surveyor to list every item. Stating the materials, styles, and manufacturers—if known—of the groups of hardware will set the tone of the boat's outfitting. For example: "Mixed aluminum and stainless steel Schaefer blocks and cleats"; "Chrome-plated bronze turnbuckles and stainless steel chainplates"; or "Bronze chocks and four-bolt hollow cleats by Wilcox (North and Judd)."

Of course, large individual pieces—anchor windlass, sheet and halyard winches, centerboard winch, boat davits, or jib furling or reefing systems (if not mentioned under running or standing rigging), ought to be described or identified well enough to leave no doubt as to what they were if lost, stolen, or destroyed. Nor am I using poetic license when I say "lost," for some very nice winches, snatch blocks, chocks, and cleats have been whipped overboard by taut lines when their fastenings were pulled out.

In accordance with the primary purpose of all surveys, the surveyor should scan every piece of hardware with a sharp eye for loose fastenings, stress cracks in underlying gelcoat, damage to the laminate, crumbled bedding compound, stains or actual drips belowdecks indicating leaks, and also wear, destructive corrosion, breakage, or other defects in the hardware itself.

Unfortunately, due to the way deck hardware is installed on almost all fiberglass production boats, it is only a matter of time before some pieces begin to loosen up and leak. That time is only a season or two in the worst cases, and I don't remember surveying any fiberglass boat in its second decade which had not had or did not need some piece or pieces of hardware tightened up, rebedded, or refastened. The most quickly loosened pieces are the bases of life line and bow or stern rail stanchions. Builders just don't seem to understand what a powerful pry bar a two- or three-foot stanchion is, working on bolts in its base that are but two or three inches apart.

A stanchion base that bolts to both deck and bulwark. (Courtesy Elen Boat Works)

A person who weighs 150 to 200 pounds lurching against a line or rail can easily develop a ton of pull on one or two base bolts. What is worse, when a stanchion is thrust against a pier with the inertia of the entire boat behind it, only the bending point of the stanchion limits the enormous forces at work on its base bolts. In the long run, the usual deck laminate will compress, bend, or crack under such forces unless they are spread over a much larger area than that covered by an ordinary nut and washer. Builders rarely spread these forces effectively, and that is why the stanchion bases on most boats can be depended upon to loosen up and develop leaks.

What is needed under innumerable pieces of hardware on the decks of today's production boats are backing plates of stiff stainless steel or bronze that will spread the pressure of the hardware bolts over a wide area. By limiting compression or distortion of the laminate, such plates limit or eliminate loosening of the hardware and leaking through the fastening holes.

I don't think there is a single recommendation I make more often in the survey of a fiberglass boat than that its deck hardware be given better backing plates.

NAVIGATION AND ELECTRONICS

With the exception of the compass, a surveyor is likely to be ambivalent about navigation and electronic equipment. It must, of course, be listed for the information of insurance companies and lenders, but it has no effect on the soundness of the craft, nor does it add much to the value, for electronic equipment on a boat depreciates very rapidly. Some of it does add to the safety of the crew, and I mention it in my reports under that heading (Safety) as well as under this one. Electronic instruments that make a boat safer include radiotelephones, EPIRBs, and radar. There are many others, of course, that add some measure of safety, but these are largely self-evident.

In the event of an accident, wreck, vandalism, or theft, it is important to have an accurate and specific list of navigation and electronic equipment. Some mass-produced items in this category don't have serial numbers, but the more intricate and expensive items do, and many of the former at least have a model name, which will allow the insurer to place a value on them.

Unfortunately, or fortunately, depending on whose part one takes, the surveyor might never see these items if the boat is in storage and the owner has taken them home for safekeeping. In that event, a list provided by the owner or the broker can be typed into the survey report, which should not fail to mention that the items were "not sighted" by the surveyor.

If no list is available and it is not known to the surveyor what equipment goes with the boat, his disclaimer should state that the report "does not contain a full inventory, and any items not mentioned, or items put aboard at a later date that would normally be included under insurance, should be listed, and the list appended hereto." The owner is thus reminded that the responsibility for updating inventory is his.

SPARS

Almost all fiberglass boats have aluminum spars. They are relatively cheap, durable, easy to maintain, and so much tougher than wooden spars that the abuse they receive at the hands of owners and boatyards alike is shocking to one brought up with wood. Nevertheless, I would be the last to believe that aluminum's present domination of the market for spars will continue indefinitely. We built fiberglass masts in my shop for our 37-foot Meadow Lark ketches as early as 1971, and I have never doubted that with a little more development, spars of a similar construction will be better than either aluminum or wood in many ways, not the least of which will be the elimination of standing rigging.

Meanwhile, properly built aluminum spars have few problems so stealthy that they cause a surveyor to lie awake worrying about missing them as he might worry about rot, delamination of glue joints, or fractures in wood. Corrosion is the natural enemy of aluminum. In the marine environment it is particularly aggressive, sometimes nibbling away entirely the heel of a mast that is sitting in bilge water. But one is not likely to overlook the effects of corrosion on aluminum unless they have been meticulously disguised, for when it strikes, the metal is quickly roughened with white powdery eruptions and pitting.

If corrosion is light and as yet confined to the surface, the surveyor will recommend a protective coating and offer suggestions for eliminating specific causes. He might point out the need for a better mast boot, a drain in a mast step that is holding water, or the removal of metals contacting the mast and causing electrolytic corrosion. A deeply eroded local section (often the base of the mast) may have to be cut out and replaced, usually with a matching section that is butted against the spar over a smaller, inside piece. This internal piece bridges the butt, serving as an internal reinforcing section or fishplate, and the original spar and the new section are machine-screwed to it. Where strength is important such repairs are not welded, because welding reduces the adjacent metal to a soft and malleable state called zero temper.

Being anodized or protective coated, the extrusion, or spar, sometimes does not corrode as soon as the cast aluminum mast steps and end plugs. The protective surface of these castings is bound to be laid open by the wear of moving parts such as outhaul and roller reefing mechanisms. Their recesses harbor salt around close-fitted rotating or sliding parts, and over an amazingly short period of disuse, corrosion "freezes" them tight. Knowing that this happens, the alert surveyor will operate every spinnaker pole end fitting, crank, slide, or hinge housed in or made of aluminum, knowing that sometimes even the newest looking part may be immovable to human hands.

Due to the nature of metal parts fastened together with tapping screws, machine screws, bolts, or pop rivets, it is not uncommon to find loose or dislodged spar fittings. I have seen more than one gooseneck end casting rattling loose in the boom extrusion, with but one or two retaining screws still hanging in there.

Whether because of an ill-advised choice for a replacement or because of the manufacturer's mistake, one very often finds steel fastenings on aluminum spars. At first these are more likely to seize up than to fall out, but even at the masthead, high above salt water, they will not last long. Replacement should be recommended.

Other details to check are the amount of wear in outhaul, lift, and halyard sheaves along with their boxes, pins, and axles, making sure that a wire or line can't ride over the edge of a sheave and jam between it and the wall of the box. Spreaders and jumper struts should be looked over for soundness as well as for the adequacy of the attachments to mast and wire(s). Wires must be seized into the groove or socket at the spreader tip, and unless there are wire or rod spreader lifts, the seizing or clamp must be tight enough to prevent spreaders from sliding down the wire. Anyone climbing the mast is more than likely to put his whole weight on a spreader or jumper.

STANDING RIGGING

Stainless steel is used almost exclusively for standing rigging in this

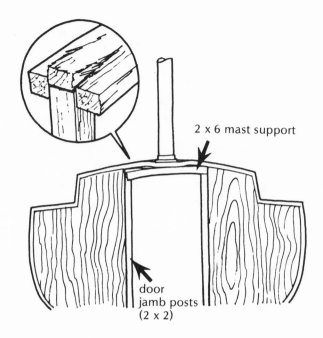

2 x 6 mast support

door
jamb posts
(2 x 2)

Here is a condition I encountered in a 26-foot pro-
duction fiberglass sloop built in 1974. A 2 x 6 under the
mast step distributed the mast's downward thrust to the
nominal 2 x 2 door jamb posts. Perhaps the shrouds
were overtightened, or perhaps the wood was of poor
quality, or perhaps the problem was the lack of foresight
in supporting the flat face of a load-bearing 2 x 6 on 2 x 2
posts, but in any case, the 2 x 6 had split as shown at the
port end, and the cabin roof was dished under the mast
step. My recommendation: Unfasten and remove the
bulkheads from the hull liner so that the 2 x 6 can be
replaced with a new piece of hardwood. Run bolts
through the new piece in a fore-and-aft direction near
either end, or face it with metal plates where it bears on
the posts. Either approach should prevent its being split
again in the future.

country, although galvanized wire is better than most U.S.
yachtsmen think. Indeed, the worst trouble I've had with it as a
surveyor has been trying to convince buyers that they needn't
arbitrarily replace every piece of it as soon as they have passed

papers on the boat. Galvanized wire usually begins to look terrible long before it is much weakened, but as soon as some buyers see any rust, they condemn the piece.

On the other hand, it is sometimes equally difficult to convince owners or buyers that some of their stainless steel wire should be replaced. Stainless is good, durable stuff, but it is not forever and it is certainly not unbreakable. It can be stretched or work hardened until its strands begin to break and its swage fittings (currently the most common attachment) let go. It is therefore necessary for the surveyor to examine each shroud, particularly at its lower end. Aside from obvious broken strands, if the spiral lay of the wire is noticeably straightened out, it has very likely been stretched beyond its yield point; it is no longer trustworthy and should be replaced. The swage socket should be examined for splits or cracks. Whether these are just starting in its top edge or rim, or extend down its side, they indicate that the socket is heading for failure.

Turnbuckles and toggles—if there are toggles—must also be scrutinized. A bend in the threaded portion of an eye or jaw, excessive wear, or even such seemingly minor details as misfitted clevis pins or missing cotter pins ought to be pointed out. Not that one's recommendations will always be taken seriously. One owner told me he hadn't had cotter pins in his turnbuckles for a dozen years because they're absolutely unnecessary. I had trouble repressing the comment that this was a remarkable discovery and that the manufacturers should be told not to provide cotter pin holes or lock nuts in the future. Then I noticed that the buyer, who had worked in a prestigious rigging loft, wasn't buying any such nonsense, and I let the subject drop.

The mast tangs and the chainplates should be inspected either at this point or during the hull survey for their condition and that of their fastenings into mast and hull.

If the boat is rigged at the time of survey, the surveyor can, of course, look into how the rigging is set up or "tuned." Thinking as a boatbuilder and surveyor, one of the worst habits I have discovered is that of setting up a gang of rigging so taut that something is bound to give, and often already has. In fiberglass production boats with deck-stepped masts, the bulkheads, corner posts, or the beams that support the mast step may be badly buckled, and I have found some parts broken under the intense downward thrust of the mast. I have also seen bulkheads pulled loose where they were fiberglassed to the hull, so that the only thing preventing attached chainplates from pulling out of the boat was the bulkhead's inability to fit through the holes in the deck. A description of what is happening or what is likely to happen to the boat should be worked into the surveyor's recommendations, for it might just convince the owner or the buyer that the rigging has been overtightened.

Sometimes a mast will have been pulled badly out of line by its rigging. In such a case the surveyor ought to make an appropriate recommendation.

RUNNING RIGGING

Since about midcentury the materials used for running rigging in this country have been almost exclusively Dacron line and 7 x 19 stainless steel wire. The changeover from Manila and other natural fibers to synthetic marine cordage was swift and sweeping, so superior were the new products.

When the boat is unrigged, it takes imagination to visualize some of the sheets and loose parts in place. Further, the surveyor may not get to see them at all, for they are often carted home by the owner or heaped in a boatyard locker amidst a ton of other gear.

Most surveyors don't let these details bother them, and as far as I know make few comments about the number of parts or leads of the lines even when the boat is fully rigged. Rather, they confine their remarks to naming the materials and hardware used and their physical condition. After all, sailors have a constant flow of information and advice at hand in yachting periodicals and books about line and hardware configurations for cruising or racing. I'm reminded of the comment one friend made when our conversation touched on a particular boating magazine. Said he, "I got so tired of the articles about sail trimming, sheet leads, and boom vangs in that rag that I let the subscription run out."

In contrast to deck-based running rigging, halyards, outhauls, and lifts are usually left in place on today's aluminum spars, which need not be unrigged for painting or varnishing. These parts are therefore accessible for inspection when the boat is in storage, although I have found the spars buried under a pile of other spars or wedged behind them in racks 20 feet off the floor. Some boatyards will dig them out or get them down for a surveyor, but others will not without a specific order from the owner or broker, because they fear, often with good reason, that they won't be paid for it. Regardless, the surveyor should sight it all, one way or another. It can be a dirty, dangerous, or discouragingly difficult job, perhaps requiring a powerful flashlight in a dark shed, but it can also be the easiest part of the survey when the spars happen to be lying on sawhorses in the sun. That's the luck of the draw in surveying.

SAILS

I keep trying to convince buyers and insurers that a boat's sails should be surveyed by a sailmaker. The trade is highly specialized, and the average surveyor has no more background than the average experienced yachtsman for judging either the quality or the condition of a sail.

A surveyor's choices are: (1) He can adamantly refuse to inspect the sails. (2) He can give his opinion along with a disclaimer that it is only that. (3) He can compare notes with the owner, or, if he is lucky, he may find that the sails have been maintained by a sailmaker who can give him their history and an accurate assessment of their condition. (4) He can simply state the maker and the age and describe the appearance of each sail—clean, dirty, new looking, patched here or frayed there—offering no opinion as to general condition or the probable amount of remaining life. Such information about details, particularly the age, seems to satisfy many buyers, insurers, or lenders, but I have trouble with it because it skirts the important questions: Is it a well-built sail? How much longer might it be expected to give good service? Does it need work now, to reinforce it before some part lets go?

As everyone knows, sails today are made of synthetic fibers woven into cloths with wonderful physical properties. These materials are vulnerable to sunlight, however, and exposure over a number of years can turn them into a substance not unlike rotted natural fibers. It is therefore very important that they be covered as much of the time as possible. The presence or absence of sail covers for boomed sails and margin cloths to shade roller furling sails are strong clues to their care. Until the day when sailcloth is immune to sunlight, it is a good idea for the surveyor to mention in his report whether or not the sails have covers.

10

Part by Part in Wood

Because wood and fiberglass are such different materials, this short chapter is needed to supplement the last long one. Short, because our part-by-part look at a boat's many systems need not be repeated.

From the day she is built, a wooden boat's hull and deck structures are beset by slow deterioration, the most common causes of which are working, weathering, rot, teredos, delaminated glue joints, broken or split wood, and wasted metal fastenings. Should she avoid shipwreck and other types of accidental death, the wooden boat will eventually succumb to some combination of these seven ailments. It is therefore a most important part of every wooden boat survey to determine which if any of them are present in what degree, and to make appropriate recommendations.

This is relatively easy when a boat's problems have reached a state as easily identified as broken ribs, loose planks, open rot pockets, or copious leaks; the true art of surveying is in the identification of hidden problems by faint symptoms, which requires a mixture of deep concentration, imagination, common sense, and almost unlimited patience. Many times, nagged by problems I might have missed or did not fully understand, I have

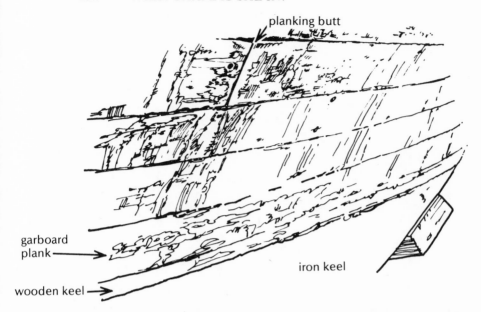

planking butt

garboard
plank

iron keel

wooden keel

A sprung planking butt, indicative of a needed refastening, a soft butt block, or both. The cracked, prominent plank seams also signal wasted fastenings, and the wide seams between garboard and wooden keel and between wooden and iron keel may mean that the keelbolts need replacing.

made from one to three return trips to a wooden boat to poke, tap, and stare at more places or to pull a few more fastenings. Whether the effort led to discovery of a previously undetected defect, to a better understanding of one not encountered before, or to the elimination of suspected problems, I never regretted it, for surveying wooden hulls and decks is a tricky business—the older, the trickier.

WORKING

"Working" refers to the slight movement of parts relative to one another. It is responsible for the creaking and groans of old boats, and it is first seen in broken paint along seams and in leaks that open up underway, subsiding when the boat is at rest. Ultimately, the results of working are seen as changes in the boat's shape: a hardening of the turn of the bilge until ribs break and planks jut outward; an acuteness of the reverse turn or "tuck" of the bilge, which sharpens until ribs break and planks angle inward; humps in the sheer resulting from shroud tension; and the hogged sheer and hollow transom of a boat whose ends have fallen, her lowered stern perhaps causing her propeller shaft(s) to bear against the bottom of the shaft log. All these and many more effects of working in older boats bring home to us the truth of the remark that a traditionally built wooden boat is "a bundle of sticks," ever ready to come apart, and that if we wish her to remain healthy we must constantly check on how well she is being held together.

WEATHERING

Some varieties of wood resist the weather better than others. As all mariners know, teak is the best weathering wood available to boatbuilders worldwide in the large sizes and quantities needed. It contains a natural oil that resists rapid saturation, drying, and rot, and it has a mineral content that gives it "tooth," resists abrasion, and dulls tools. Long prized for use on decks, where it gives an excellent nonskid surface wet or dry, bare teak is now plastered indiscriminately over the inside as well as the outside of production boats, because, expensive as it is, it eliminates the greater expense of a protective finish and is generally accepted by owners as an attractive, low maintenance material.

In the long term, no variety of wood, teak included, can withstand weathering. Inevitably, although at different rates to be sure, all wood will be warped, twisted, checked, rent, or eroded by exposure to the weather. The surveyor often feels compelled to point out—a bit sharply—the folly of neglecting to protect wood surfaces.

ROT

While weathered wood may be beat up and sad looking, rotten wood is sick, and the surveyor can hardly stress immediate treatment strongly enough. Looking back on my experience, 80 percent of the

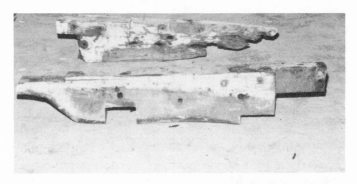

Water lodging beneath them rotted both these engine beds and the adjacent planking. (Courtesy Elen Boat Works)

wooden boats that were turned down by buyers after survey simply had too much rot in them. What is frustrating about it is that we have the know-how and the products to prevent rot or to stop it dead on discovery, yet too often it is let go until it has ruined a part or parts of the boat.

Some owners just never get around to doing anything about rot until their boat is desperately, even terminally ill, then they suddenly wake up and spring into action with putty, paint, and a "For Sale" sign. My introduction to painted-over rot was the survey of an elderly Friendship sloop about 30 years ago. Tapping and probing brought to my attention one sickeningly soft area after another under her heavily painted finish. Being young, brash, and new to surveying, I kept sinking my pick to the hilt to prove to myself as well as to the equally young buyer how much of the wood was disintegrated. The holes my pick left got me bitterly scolded by the sly and shameless old owner, who, disarmingly, happened to be a minister of the gospel. Said he, "You ruined my paint job!" A year later I also got scolded by the client, who had bought the boat in complete disregard of my disparaging report and was now hurting to the tune of thousands of dollars in repairs. Said he, "You shouldn't have let me buy her."

Sometimes a surveyor can't win, but eventually he does learn to locate rot without ruining the paint job. He learns the signs. He sees the slight blistered look of paint with moist wood under it, perhaps notices tiny beads of moisture on a plank or stem surface, hears the change to a dull thud as he taps the area with, say, the plastic handle of a screwdriver, and uses nothing sharper than that to probe the wood unless he can find a seam or a flake of loose paint where he can insert his pick without leaving an unsightly hole in the finish. But the most important result of experience is the knowledge of where rot is most likely to be found. In general, there is likely to be rot wherever moisture lingers, particularly where fresh water leaks in and stands. Rot will take hold under deck hardware or trim that is not well bedded. It likes a crack, a seam, a butt joint, or the hole of a wasted fastening—any frequently dampened, slow-drying spot.

The corners of cabin trunks and deckhouses are notorious for leaks that won't stop and eventually breed rot. An important reason is that the sides and ends are usually wide boards laid on their long edges. These swell and shrink along the vertical axis, moving up and down on the corner posts, which, with their grain running vertically, change height very little if at all. As the moisture content of the wood changes, the deckhouse sides and ends either shrink and are held off the deck by the corner posts, or they swell, jacking the corner posts off the deck.

Window ledges or rabbets; dirt-clogged hatch gutters and toerail scuppers; the upturned grain of stemhead, bitts, rudderhead, or even masthead; and the hard-to-seal deck joints adjacent to stem, bulwark stanchions, and covering boards can all harbor rot when water accumulates in, under, between, or against them.

The hood ends of the planking are forever working faintly open where they meet the stem's rabbet and the transom's edges, developing a tendency to take in fresh water. Too often there is little or no circulation of air to dry up wetness on the interior quickly, and bows and sterns are notorious for rotting out.

Belowdecks, butt blocks will rot if leaky butts, sometimes themselves turning soft, keep things damp. This is especially true in the topsides, where the dampness is from fresh water, which is much, much more dangerous to wood than salt water. Ribs, sawn frames, and floor timbers will rot where their feet rest constantly in brackish bilge water or where silted cracks between parts stay moist. Cracks or checks in the top of a keel are a worry, for they collect dirt, which keeps them moist and invites infection. A rotten keel is the biggest single problem a wooden boat can have.

Ice in the winter pushes the stealer planks of this boat off the back rabbet of the sternpost, and dirt settling there holds the planks out in the summer. The area should be cleaned out, dried out, and refastened before rot spreads.

Two of the most easily overlooked rot prone areas are the top faces of deck beams and the outboard faces of ribs or frames. Wetness migrating through seams or the holes of wasted fastenings to lodge between these members and the decking or planking is not quickly dried out, especially when it can continue on into the timber along those fastenings or any splits that might be in it. Kept dank by repeated trickles, a streak of rot develops down the timber's unseen face, eventually converting that member to a hollow shell. Frequently, the three visible faces of the rib or beam will give no hint of the wasted core until planks or decking staves come loose and new fastenings can find no solid wood. To probe for this condition one can enter from the exterior through a fastening hole with an ice pick, or from the interior by sliding a thin, stiff wire between the timber and a loose plank or stave. The wire is bent in a curve so that it will turn down into the center of the timber should that area be soft enough to accept it.

TEREDOS (SHIP WORMS)

It may be because there are fewer wooden boats, but I, for one, don't seem to find as much worm damage on boats today as I did 20 or 30 years ago. Nevertheless, when I do find damage it usually turns out that the little monsters gained access to the wood through the same old places:

1) Through the rudderport or shaft log, if not metal lined, because the rudder stock or propeller shaft may rub some antifouling paint off the walls, and also because never, never does every last inch of these parts get painted.

2) Into the hollow after face of a sternpost or skeg and, if wood, the convex leading edge of the rudder that fits there.

3) Through the recesses or countersunk bolt holes in the bottom of a wooden keel, where a wooden plug or some putty may have fallen out or where the painter failed to look and apply his brush diligently enough.

4) Through any area that rests on blocking or support pads and as a result gets launched without fresh antifouling paint.

5) Through any crack, crevice, or scratch into which antifouling paint did not penetrate.

6) Should a boat settle below her painted waterline, through any portion of the topsides that is underwater for more than a week or two during the local "worm season."

DELAMINATED GLUE JOINTS

During and just after World War II, a number of "waterproof" glues became available to boatbuilders. That these glues did not always make a permanently waterproof joint has become more and more evident in the years since. I dislike harping about foreign imports, but some of them have been terrible in the way their glue joints have held up. There have been innumerable imports whose laminated stems, keels, deadwoods, scarfs, wooden masts, and even entire plywood skins have eventually come unstuck. Not that we haven't had similar products in this country, but perhaps because most U.S. builders jumped from traditional nonglued constructions

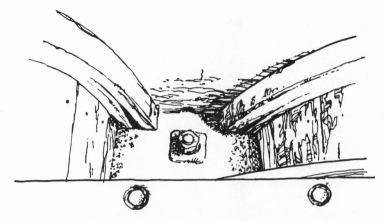

This drawing was made from a photograph looking into the bilge of an imported wooden yawl. The heels of the laminated ribs are separating where they are perpetually wet or damp. With a better glue this would not have happened.

directly into fiberglass without trying various glued-seam or cold-molded techniques, or perhaps because we had more truly waterproof glues and plywood available sooner, we seem to have escaped much of the delamination that has showed up with discouraging punctuality in many imports.

Hopefully, wholesale delamination is mostly in the past and will not affect late models so pervasively. Still, the best of glues can be handled carelessly or, being chemicals, can be miscompounded. Sometimes I wonder if I'm alone in this, but I do believe that there are varieties of wood, combinations of grain direction and thickness, and environments that will cause failure of a glue joint no matter what glue is used. As long as I'm surveying, I'll keep looking for failing glue joints.

BROKEN OR SPLIT WOOD

There are two ways that wood fails under stress: by breaking off across the grain or by splitting along the direction of the grain. In boats, breaks across the grain are commonly caused by stretching or overbending the wood, as when planking swells enough to snap off

The deadwood juts out past the after slope of this iron keel because the iron bolts within it, growing bigger with rust over the years, have split the ends of the timbers.

ribs, or when floor timbers transmit the bending forces of a ballast keel to the much smaller ribs that are bolted to them, causing the ribs to break, or when floors themselves are so strained by a mast forced down on its step by shrouds, headstay, and perhaps a hydraulic backstay tensioner that they break apart right down the line of their drifts or bolts to the keel.

Splits, on the other hand, are most often caused by a fastening forced into an undersized hole or no hole at all, or by a row of fastenings along a single line of the wood's grain. Splits are induced in the laps of lapstrake planking by repeated fastening along the same grain; they are created in wide planks and wide keels as the wood dries severely between widely spaced fastenings or keelbolts; and they appear in heavy timber, including solid spars, as the outer wood shrinks around its own heartwood.

Of course, breaks are a partial or complete failure of the wood proportionate to the fraction of the cross section that is parted. This is not necessarily true of splits, and especially of drying checks, either of which may or may not affect the function of the stick. Unless the split is deep enough to threaten to make two sticks of one, or is angled across the stick, thus threatening a break, the greatest problem with splits or checks is the danger that rot will breed in them.

WASTED METAL FASTENINGS

When planking breaks the paint over its seams, when planks are loose or the edge of one juts out past another, or when a crack grows between the ballast keel and the wooden keel or between backbone members, then the fastenings are to blame. Some might respond to tightening, but most will have been wasted away by rust or corrosion or will be bedded in wood that has been attacked by the by-products of the fastenings' electrolysis and has thus grown soft with "rust sickness."

If wasted fastenings can be easily removed and replaced, a boat can be given a new life through refastening. Unfortunately, it is sometimes very difficult or destructive to surrounding wood to remove fastenings, despite the fact that they are not holding well. When removal is frustrating and time-consuming, the temptation is simply to leave them there and add more fastenings. That's all right if there is plenty of wood left in the plank and in the frame, so that adding more holes won't weaken either member too much. Even if there is room, however, the old fastenings are still an ongoing danger in that, as they disintegrate further, they may begin to leak. While any pump can keep up with a few fastening holes, few pumps can keep up with some hundreds of them, so there could be trouble and often is. Therefore, I believe the surveyor should investigate a refastening very carefully and report the potential problems related to it.

Meanwhile, if the boat doesn't break her paint on the seams, if no planks are loose or jutting out, and if all planking is tight against frames and floors inside and smoothly contoured outside, she does not yet have a fastening problem. I don't care if she was fastened 50 years ago, the problem is not yet upon her. If you don't believe your eyes, get permission from the owner and pull out a few fastenings (if they will come). Really, though, the outwardly visible signs tell the story.

WHEN IT'S FIBERGLASS-COVERED WOOD

No sooner did fiberglass begin to appear as a boatbuilding material than it began to find use as a covering on wooden boats. It took the place of canvas on decks and housetops throughout the boatbuilding industry. During the same period, a handful of production builders and innumerable custom builders also turned out fiberglass-covered wooden hulls.

Unfortunately, the new material seemed (and was, in some ways) so much tougher than canvas that it was usually applied more thinly than it should have been. The results are everywhere to be seen on these boats in their declining years: fiberglass-covered decks agape, the coverings on rounded housetop edges split open like roasted hot dogs, and patches of covering missing entirely from hull bottoms. None of this would have happened had a more appropriate thickness of fiberglass been mechanically fastened to the wood. Some such coverings are 20 years old now, and it seems they will last indefinitely.

The surveyor should be on the lookout that a fiberglass covering is not letting water through. In a typical sequence of events leading to complete failure, a thin covering lets a bit of water seep through at a worn spot or a virtually invisible fracture of the resin where it has been banged by some hard object. Once in, water swells the wood, splits and loosens the glass from its surfaces, and creates a lingering wet spot. If it goes unnoticed, the wet spot eventually becomes infected. As a "rot pocket," it stealthily expands until it is finally recognized as an incipient disaster area. The alert surveyor will, presumably, be able to discover and warn that a thin covering is in need of repair, or perhaps some additional layers, before the underlying woodwork is seriously damaged. After all, looking closely at everything and knowing what big problems can develop from little things is at the core of the surveyor's art.

Index

Air conditioning, 137-138
Air-intake valve, 22, 111
Alcohol fueled stove, 134, 135
Alligatoring, 89
Aluminum hardware, 83-84, 145, 148
American Boat and Yacht Council, 16
American Safety Products, 139
Anchors, 139
Antifouling paint, 130, 157
Antifreeze, 112, 120
Appraisal, 3, 7-9, 11-12, 143
Athwartship cracks (in hull laminate), 97-98
Auxiliary generator, 112, 126-127
Awlgrip spray finish, 73

Backing plates for deck hardware, 35, 94, 142-143
Ball valve, frozen, 131-132
Balsa-cored hull, 97
Battery, 38, 113, 124-125
Bearings, 73-74, 102-105, 107, 109, 110-111
Belt-driven bilge pump, high-capacity, 133
Bilge pumps, 22, 35, 38, 132-133
Bilges, 113
Blistering, gelcoat, 45-48, 154
Boat brokers, 4-5
Boat pox, 44-48, 85
Boatyard operators, 4, 18
Book price, 11
Brass hardware, 132
Breakouts, gelcoat, 94-96
Broken wood, 71-72, 158-160
Brokers, boat, 4-5
Bronze seacock, 131
Bronze through hull, 129-130
Built-in self destruction, 70, 72
Buyer participation, 28-29, 33-34
Buyer's options, 53
Buyer's survey, 7-9, 10, 11, 16, 33, 39-43, 62-68, 80-82, 85-87, 113-114, 143

CNG. *See* Compressed natural gas
Camping stove, 137
Cannister-muffler, 118, 120
Centerboards, 99-101
Centerline joints, 97-98, 102
Checklist, survey, 9-10, 13-15, 33
Checks, drying, 155, 159-160
Coast Guard regulations, 12, 48, 113, 121, 123, 124
Cockpit lockers, 34-36, 73

Cold-molded construction, 58, 60, 158
Compressed natural gas, 134, 137
Condition survey. *See* Buyer's survey
Conrad, Joseph, 2
Cooling systems, 112
Copper exhaust system, 116
Copper tubing through hull, 130
Cordage, synthetic marine, 148
Cores, waterlogged, 96-97, 155-156
Corrosion, 83-84, 99, 102, 107, 120, 121, 127, 129, 131, 141, 144, 145, 160
Cosmetic condition, 88-89, 95
Cost, survey, 3
Cracks, 21, 33, 34, 78, 83, 89-94, 97-98, 107, 120, 141, 155. *See also* Split wood
Crazing, 89

Dacron line, 148
Deck condition, 30-32, 33-37, 49-53, 72-76, 78, 88, 93-96, 155
Deck hardware, 35, 71, 78, 83-84, 140, 141-143, 155, 159
Delamination, 50-53, 72-73, 75, 92-94, 141, 157-158
Delrin through hull, 22, 37, 101, 129-130
Depthsounder, 22, 39, 130-131
Dezincifying, 132
Diaphragm hand pump, 133
Diesel fuel, 113, 116, 121, 124
Dry storage, 51
Drying checks, 155, 159-160

EPIRB. *See* Emergency position-indicating radio beacon
Electric pump, 132
Electrical systems, 35, 113, 125-129, 135
Electrolytic problems, 26, 84, 101, 107, 127, 128, 129, 130, 131, 144, 145, 160
Electronic equipment, 143-144
Emergency position-indicating radio beacon, 140-141, 143
Engine flooding, 118
Engine startup, inadvertent, 107
Engines, 35, 36, 111-114
Eruptions, white powdery, 144
Escrow agreement, 36, 99
Exhaust systems, 22, 35, 36-37, 83, 114-120, 130
Explosions, 120, 124
Exterior condition, hull, 19-28, 30, 44-48, 88-93
Extinguishers, fire, 138-139

Fiberglass advantages, 58-60
Fiberglass boat surveying, 88-150
Fiberglass coverings, 58, 72-73, 161
Fiberglass laminate condition, 19-21, 30, 34, 35, 45-48, 72-73, 78-79, 82, 84-85, 88-95
Fiberglass sap, 77-87
Fiberglass skin disease. *See* Boat pox
Fiberglass tubing through hull, 101, 129
Fill plates, 36, 121-122
Financial risks, 2

Fire extinguishers, 138-139
Fire Protection Standards for Pleasure and Commercial Motor Craft (National Fire Protection Association), 16
Fires, 120, 124, 128
Flame arrestor, 122, 130
Flashlight, 16
Fouling, 130
Fractures, remote laminate, 97
Freezer systems, 138
Fuel systems, 112-113, 120-124
Fuel tank, 22, 36, 111, 121
Fumes, gasoline, 121, 125, 135, 137
Fuses, 126

Galvanized wire, 146-147
Gasoline fueled stove, 137
Gasoline fuels, 113, 116, 121, 124, 134, 137. *See also* Fumes
Gate valve, frozen, 131
Gelcoat, porous, 46, 85
Generator, auxiliary, 112, 126-127
Glue joints, delaminated, 31-32, 71, 97-98, 102, 157-158
Glued-seam construction, 71, 158
Glues, 71, 72, 157-158
Grease cups, 111
Ground tackle, 139-140
Grounding, electrical, 35, 121, 127-128, 135
Grounding damage, 19-21

Halon gas extinguisher, 138-139
Halonite, 139
Hammer, 16
Hand, William, 123
Hardware, deck, 35, 71, 78, 83-84, 140, 141-143, 155, 159
Hardware, inadequate, 28, 30, 31-32, 140, 145
Hazard identification, 12-16
Heaters, 134-137
Hull exterior condition, 19-29, 30, 44-48, 88-93
Hull interior condition, 30, 38-39, 79, 96-101
Hydraulic systems, 106-107

IOR production auxiliary sloop survey, 18-43
Icebox, 137
Imported boats, 69-76
Imron spray finish, 73
Insurance agents, marine, 4
Insurance survey, 3, 7-9, 12-16, 139, 143
Interior condition, hull, 30, 38-39, 79, 96-101
Internal injuries, 21
Inventory, 16, 140, 143-144
Iroko decking, 49-53
Isolation transformer, 128-129, 135

Joints: delaminated glue, 31-32, 71, 97-98, 102, 157-158; mitered, 71

Keels, 19, 21, 38, 98-99, 100, 110, 155
Kerosene fueled stove, 134, 135
Kershaw, Robert N., 9, 13-15
Kindling points, 138

LPG. *See* Liquefied petroleum gas
Leaks. *See* Watertightness problems
Lifesaving equipment, 140-141
Liquefied petroleum gas, 125, 134, 135-137
Lockers, cockpit, 34-36, 73
Lovett electric submersible bilge pump, 132
Lubrication problems, 107, 111, 131

Manila line, 148
Manufacturer's responsibility, 32, 76
Margin cloths, 150
Marine growth, 50, 130
Marine-Tex putty, 46, 89
Martec propeller, folding, 25
Measuring rule, 17
Mechanical systems, 106-107
Metal fastenings, wasted, 145, 155, 156, 160-161
Mirror, 17
Mitered joints, 71
Moisture, trapped, 45. *See also* Rot
Monel hardware, 71
Moorings, 139
Murphy's Law, 96, 137

National Fire Protection Association, 16
Navigational systems, 143-144
Navy hand pump, 133
Novie keel, hollow, 110

Oil fueled stove, 134, 135
Oil spills, 113
Overloaded circuits, 125, 126

PFD. *See* Personal flotation device
Personal flotation device, 140
Pigtails, 128
Pitting, 107, 144
Plank-on-frame construction, 58, 72
Pliers, 17
Polarity indicator, 128, 135
Pop rivets, 31-32
Power, shore, 127-129
Pox, boat, 44-48, 85
Practical Sailor, The, 76
Preliminary survey, 3
Price, book, 11
Probe, 16
Propeller, 25-26, 35, 107, 111

Propulsion gear, 25-26, 35, 107-111, 112, 157
Puddling, 50-51, 155
Pumps, 132-133, 137
Putties, 21, 45-46, 89

Radar devices, 143
Radios, 140-141, 143
Rattling noise, 107
Refastening problems, 56-58, 160
Refrigeration systems, 137-138
Resin, undercured, 96
Responsibility: manufacturer's, 32, 76; surveyor's, 54, 80, 112, 124, 149
Rigging: running, 148-149; standing, 144, 145-148
Rivets, pop, 31-32
Rodes, 139
Rot pocket, 161
Rot problems, 50-53, 55-64, 137, 149-150, 153-156, 160, 161
Rudder, 26-28, 33, 35, 73-74, 83, 101-104
Rule, measuring, 17
Rules and Regulations for Recreational Boats (Coast Guard), 12
Running Rigging, 148-149
Rust sickness, 73-74, 120, 121, 125, 129, 130, 132, 141, 147, 160

Sabb feathering propeller and shaft unit, 111
Safety devices, 140-141, 143
Safety survey. *See* Insurance survey
Sail covers, 150
Sailmakers, 149
Sails, 149-150
Schwab, Louie, 116
Screwdrivers, 17
Seacocks, 34, 37, 129-132
Selector switch, 125
Self-destruction, built-in, 70, 72
Sequence, survey, 33, 88
Settling, 157
Shaft, propeller, 35, 107, 111
Ship worms. *See* Teredos
Shock, electrical, 134
Shore power, 127-129
Short circuits, 125, 126
Siphon break, 133
Sniffer, gas, 137
Solid fuels, 134, 135
Sounding, 16-17
Spars, 35, 39, 144-145, 147-148
Split wood, 158-160
Stack exhaust system, 116-117, 120
Stanchions, 33, 141-142
Standards and Recommended Practices for Small Craft (American Boat and Yacht Council), 16
Standing rigging, 144, 145-148
Star cracks, 34, 89-92, 93

Static electricity, 121
Steel wire, stainless, 71, 83, 84, 145-146, 147, 148
Steering systems, 35, 104-107
Stern bearing, 107, 109, 110-111
Stop bolts, 28, 30
Storage, dry, 51
Stoves, 134-137
Street, Donald, 132
Stress cracks, 21, 33, 34, 78, 89, 92-94, 141, 158
Struts, 109, 145
Stuffing box, 35, 36, 73-74, 103, 107, 109-111
Style, surveyor's, 10-11
Sump pump, 137
Survey: aborted, 29; definition of, 7; need for, 2-3; preliminary, 3
Survey checklist, 9-10, 13-15, 33
Survey cost, 3
Survey sequence, 33, 88
Survey types, 7-9
Surveyor selection, 3-6, 77
Surveyor's responsibility, 54, 80, 112, 124, 143, 149
Switches, 125, 126, 132-133
Synthetic marine cordage, 148

Tapered-barrel seacock, 131
Teak wood, 74-75, 153
Telltale Compass, The, 76
Teredos, 157
Thiokol seam compound, 50, 52
Threaded through hull, 129-130
Through hulls, 22, 34, 37, 38-39, 101, 129-132, 133, 137
Tiller steering systems, 104
Tools, surveying, 16-17
Trial agreement, 36
Tuning, rig, 147-148

Value survey. *See* Appraisal
Vaporproof master battery switch, 38, 125
Varnish rejection, 73
Vent, fuel tank, 22, 35, 122-123
Ventilation, 33, 64, 111, 124, 155
Vibration problems, 83, 125, 130
Voltage problems, 125, 127-129

Warning light, 136-137
Wasted metal fastenings, 145, 155, 156, 160-161
Water-lift exhaust system, 36-37, 117-118, 120
Waterlines, 19, 157
Watertightness problems, 30-31, 55-61, 77-78, 96-97, 99, 100, 101, 112, 120, 130, 132, 141,
    160
Weathering problems, 77, 153
Wheel steering systems, 35, 104-105
Wicking, 96
Wiring systems, 35, 37-38, 74, 106, 113, 125-126, 135

Wood: broken, 71-72, 158-160; fiberglass-covered, 58, 72-73, 161; split, 158-160
Wooden boat surveying, 151-161
Working problems, 152-153. *See also* Watertightness problems
Worms, ship. *See* Teredos
Wrenches, 17

Yield points, 147

Zero temper, 145